Valentines for the Eclectic Collector

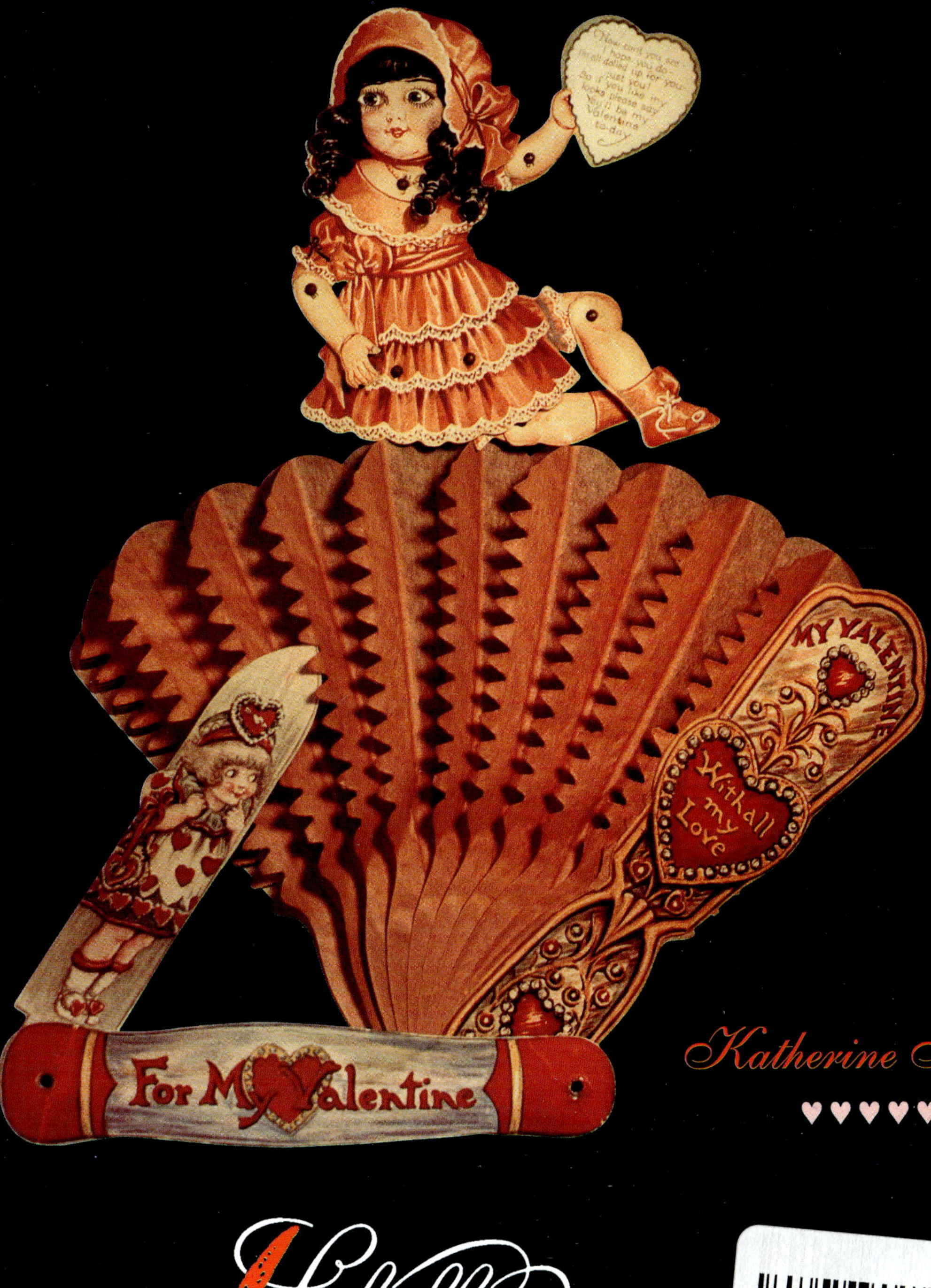

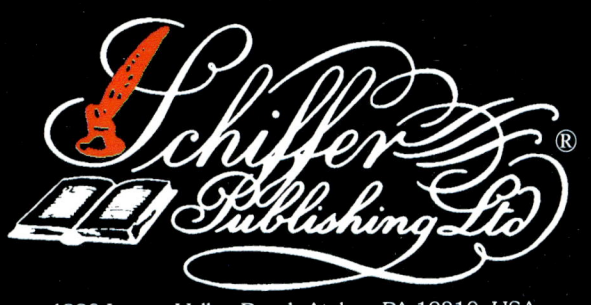

Katherine Kreider

♥♥♥♥♥♥

Schiffer Publishing Ltd ®

4880 Lower Valley Road, Atglen, PA 19310 USA

I0384125

♥ Dedication ♥

To all of the Great Lovers of the world, Cleopatra, Rudolph Valentino, Errol Flynn, Clark Gable, Marlena Dietrich, George Burns and Gracie Allan (who collected Valentines), and J. David Kreider (my handsome husband). Without the help of these great romantics Valentine's Day would have perished years ago. Therefore, *Valentines for the Eclectic Collector* is dedicated to ALL THE ROMANTICS OF THE WORLD!

Copyright © 1999 by Katherine Kreider
Library of Congress Catalog Card Number: 99-62203

All rights reserved. No part of this work may be reproduced or used in any form or by any means—graphic, electronic, or mechanical, including photocopying or information storage and retrieval systems—without written permission from the copyright holder.
"Schiffer," "Schiffer Publishing Ltd. & Design," and the "Design of pen and ink well" are registered trademarks of Schiffer Publishing Ltd.

Photographs by Katherine Kreider
Designed by Bonnie M. Hensley
Type set in Shelley Allegro BT/Korinna BT

ISBN: 0-7643-0917-X
Printed in China
1 2 3 4

Published by Schiffer Publishing Ltd.
4880 Lower Valley Road
Atglen, PA 19310
Phone: (610) 593-1777; Fax: (610) 593-2002
E-mail: Schifferbk@aol.com
Please visit our web site catalog at **www.schifferbooks.com**

In Europe, Schiffer books are distributed by Bushwood Books
6 Marksbury Avenue Kew Gardens
Surrey TW9 4JF England
Phone: 44 (0)181 392-8585; Fax: 44 (0)181 392-9876
E-mail: Bushwd@aol.com

This book may be purchased from the publisher.
Include $3.95 for shipping. Please try your bookstore first.
We are interested in hearing from authors with book ideas on related subjects.
You may write for a free printed catalog.

♥ Contents ♥

Introduction—5
Usage Guide—6
Valentine Categories—7
Chapter 1. Novelty—8
Chapter 2. Deltiology—83
Chapter 3. OEAs: Other Ephemeral Artifacts—107
Third Top Ten Most Asked Questions—126
Glossary—126
Bibliography—128
Index—128

CHARACTER COPYRIGHTS AND TRADEMARKS

This is in no way intended to infringe on the intellectual property rights of any party. All products, brands, characters, and names represented are trademarks or registered trademarks of their respective companies, all rights reserved.

The information in this book is derived from the author' s independent research and is not authorized, furnished or approved by any of the companies mentioned in this book.

Below are all trademarked characters and titles exhibited in this book, listed by the companies which own them (copyrights may apply).

Avon™
Marjorie Henderson Buell: Alvin©, LuLu©, Tubby Tompkins© Wilbur Van Snobbe©
Milton Caniff: Terry and the Pirates™
Disney/The Walt Disney Company: Bashful™, Blue Fairy™, Cleo™, Clarabell™, Daisy Duck™, Donald Duck™, Dopey™, Gepetto™, Goofy™, Jiminy Cricket™, Mickey Mouse™, Minnie Mouse™, Pinocchio™, Pluto™, Snow White and the Seven Dwarfs™, Wiley Fox™, Winnie the Pooh™
Felix the Cat Productions: Felix the Cat™
Hall Syndicate: Dennis the Menace™, Mr. Wilson™, Margaret™, Ruff™, Henry and Alice Mitchell™, Joey™,
Hanna-Barbera: Baby Puss™, Bamm Bamm™, Barney Rubble™, Betty Rubble™, The Flintstones™, Fred Flintstone™, Pebbles™, Puss™, Snagglepuss™, Wilma Flintstone™, Yogi Bear™
Hearst Syndicate: Archy(cockroach)™, Bringing Up Father™, Flip™, Gloomy Gus™, Happy Hooligan™, Ignatz™, Jiggs™, Krazy Kat™, Lord Montmorency™, Maggie™, Dinty Moore™, Nora™, Officer Pup™, The Kewpies™,
International Feature Services: Abie The Agent™
John F. Dillie Co. Syndicate: Buck Rogers™
Rudolph Dirks: der Captain©, der Inspector©, Fritz©, Hans©, Lena©, Mamma©, Rollo Rhubarb©, Miss Twiddle©, The Katzenjammer Kids©
Frank King: Bill©, Auntie Blossom©, Corky©, Doc©, Gasoline Alley©, Judy©, Nina©, Skeezix©, Uncle Avery©, Uncle Walt©

King Features: Betty Boop™, Blondie™, Flash Gordon™, Henry™, Henrietta™, Mickey Mouse™, The Newlyweds™, Olive Oyl™, Pete The Tramp™, Popeye™, Prince Valiant™, Snookums™, Swee'Pea™, Tillie The Toiler™, Wimpy™
Loew's Inc: Wizard of Oz™
William Moulton Marston: Capt. Steve Trevor©, Diana Prince©, Wonder Woman©
Winsor McCay: Flip©, Impy©, King Morpheous©, Nemo©, Doctor Phil©
McDonalds™
McNaught Syndicates: Eppy Hogg™, Grandma Demon Chaperone™, Katrinka™, Little Woo-Woo Wortle™, Mickey McGuire™, Mr. Bang™, Snake-Tongue Tompkins™, Skippy and Trolley™, Toonerville Folks™, Uncle Chew Wilson™
McClure Syndicate: Clark Kent™, Lois Lane™, Jimmy Olsen™, Superman™, Perry White™
National Periodical Publications: Batman™, Catwoman™, Joker™, Penguin™, Robin, the Boy Wonder™
New York News Syndicate: Bonnie Braids™, B. O. Plenty™, Jr. Tracy™, Dick Tracy™, Gravel Gertie™, Pat Patton™, Sparkle Plenty™, Tess Truehart™
Richard F. Outcault : Buster Brown©, Buddy Tucker©, Mary Jane©, Tige©, The Yellow Kid©
Paramount Pictures: Betty Boop™
Pillsbury: Doughboy™
Charles Edward Schultze: Foxy Grandpa©
Sidney Smith: Andy Gump™, Chester Gump™, Ching Chow™, Mama De Stross™, Min Gump™, Tilda the maid™, Uncle Bin™, Widow Zander™
United Artists Pictures, Inc.: Pink Panther™
United Feature Syndicate, Inc.: Charlie Brown™, Daisy Mae™, Cicero™, Ella Cinders™, Franklin™, Li'l Abner™, Linus™, Lucy™, Mutt and Jeff™, Peanuts™, Peppermint Patty™, Pig Pen™, Prince Valiant™, Sally™, Schroeder™, Snoopy™, Tarzan™
Frank Willard: Kayo© Mamie©, Moon Mullins©, Lord Plushbottom©, Emmy Schmaltz©, Uncle Willie©

We regret any omissions caused by error or the absence of identifying information on any artifact.

Thank You's

My Special Valentine Thank You to the following contributors to
Valentines for the Eclectic Collector

♥ ♥ ♥ ♥ ♥

♥Ron Hagg and Larry: from Temple, Pennsylvania, otherwise known as "H & H." Thank you both for your dedication to the preservation of the Victorian Era, from Valentines to houses.

♥Wayne Herstad: from Tacoma, Washington, the *best* chiropractor in the Great North West. He still has time to pursue his passion of Valentine collecting. Many heartfelt thanks for your wonderful additions to *Valentines for the Eclectic Collector.*

♥Dorice and Herb Honberger: from Mt. Joy, Pennsylvania, two of the smartest and most fashion forward antiques dealers I know. Thanks for adding to the documentation of the Valentine. You are now in the Library of Congress!

♥Postmaster Rick Brodeaux and Cindy Rhoades from the Chamber of Commerce: from Valentine, Nebraska, for sharing Valentine's history and cachets so everyone can have the opportunity to learn a bit more about the city with a "Big Heart" and partake in the Valentine, Nebraska, remailing program.

♥Sandra and Kent Renshaw: from Freeland, Washington, who emulate the true meaning of Valentine's Day everyday! Thank you for upholding the standards of ephemera collecting as it should be and for sharing some of your artifacts with the world!

♥Judy Smith from Lancaster, Pennsylvania, for her eclectic additions to *Valentines for the Eclectic Collector.*

♥Sandi Swanson from Seattle, Washington, for her inspiration and fortitude in life and for her devotion to the preservation of Valentine postcards with telephone motifs and telephone ephemera!

♥My apologizes to anyone I have missed. Whether you are listed above or not, you ALL deserve to be commended! Please give each of yourselves a big Valentine's hug.

♥ ♥ ♥ ♥ ♥

♥ Introduction ♥

Valentines for the Eclectic Collector, refers to my third book in a series of photographic essays documenting the Valentine card. It also describes three chapters in this third volume of Valentines: Novelties, Other Ephemeral Artifacts, and Postcards. This trilogy of Valentine chapters represents the eclectic side of Valentine collecting, from party favors to paper dolls to Valentine catalogs. Samples from each of these chapters need to be added to a collection if the collector wishes to represent a total retrospective of the Valentine card. One of the most asked for additions in this trilogy of Valentines is the chapter on postcards. So with the help of Sandra and Kent Renshaw, owners of Potlatch Traders, in Freeland, Washington, and Sandra Swanson, from Seattle, Washington, who graciously allowed me to photograph postcards from their personal collections, this chapter was accomplished.

In *Valentines With Values*, *One Hundred Years of Valentines*, and *Valentines for the Eclectic Collector* I have begun to document the "sets" and "series" of Valentine cards. There is so much work to be done that I encourage everyone to please write or call me with any additional information you might have to help complete the "sets" and "series" already represented in this trilogy. This trilogy of books is only the tip of the heart! My motto is: Save the Valentine! In our home Valentine's Day is every day of the year!

Please send your cards and letters to: Katherine Kreider, Kingsbury Antiques, P.O. Box 7957, Lancaster, PA 17604-7957 or call (717)892-3001, or stop our booth #315 at, Stoudtburg Antiques Center (better known as Black Angus) Rt. 72 in Adamstown, PA. I look forward to hearing from everyone! Happy Valentine's Day,

—Katherine Kreider

♥ A Usage Guide ♥

These are styles of cards that are identifiable among the various categories of Valentine cards.

DIMENSIONAL: this style of card can have one or more dimensions. When pricing this type of card, it is very important to include the height, width, and depth.

FLAT: this style of card is not raised, does not move, or have any dimension to it, it has a level surface.

GREETING CARD: this style of card is always folded into several folds and opens up vertically or horizontally.

MECHANICAL-FLAT: a card with one or more moving part.

POSTCARD: a flat cardboard type card measuring 3.5" x 5", known as the standard size sent through the postal system with a hand-written message on the back.

♥ Valentine Categories ♥

The following list of major categories will always appear in one of the previously mentioned card styles.

Advertising: Bon Ami™, Frigidaire™, Buster Brown™, any card advertising a particular product.

Artist Signed: Ellen Clapsaddle, Grace Drayton, Ernest Nister, this is when an artist signature appears on a card.

Celebrities: a movie, radio, or television personality such as: Charlie Chaplin, Jimmy Durante, or Joe Penner.

Comic Character: Snow White™, Pink Panther™, Pete the Tramp™, any card with a comic strip character or cartoon character on it.

Ethnic: large group of people with common traits, customs, language or social views.

Hold-to-Light: a card that has a tissue or cellophane backing, covering a city of lights, the port holes of a steamship, etc. When the card is held to the light, it looks as though you switched on a light.

Novelties: Cards that have a playful use to them. Within this category you also will find gift-giving Valentine cards. These cards might have bottles of perfume attached, hankies, or any item that represents a token of love.

Transportation: cars, trains, steamships, carriages, airplanes, etc., used as the focal point of a card.

Within the above major categories there are many sub-categories as well. Remember the list is endless: animals, children, fairy tales, flowers, gum, musical instruments, nursing, scouting, smoking, sports, war, etc.

Please refer to the following definitions and abbreviations to understand the captions under each Valentine pictured.

CAPTION ABBREVIATIONS
AS—Artist signed
D—Dimensional (one dimension only)
F—Flat
F with D—Flat with Dimension
GC—Greeting card
HCPP—-Honey comb paper puff
M—Mechanical
MF—Mechancial-Flat
MIG—Made in Germany
N—Novelty
ND—Novelty with Dimension
NF—Novelty-Flat
NGC—Novelty Greeting Card
NMF—Novelty Mechanical-Flat
PIG—Printed in Germany

CONDITION TYPES

M—Mint: uncirculated
NM—Near Mint: was circulated and usually has a signature written on the back, but there are no creases, pin holes, tears, restoration, etc.
EX—Excellent: the surface of the card has no visible problems, but restoration work could have been done on the back.
G—Good: creases, fading, pin holes, etc., could appear on this card, along with some restoration work on the front and back of the card.
P—Poor: falling apart, torn, possibly a parts piece for restoration work, possibly could be restored.

The following example of a caption used in this book has been expanded to help readers use the abbreviation system with ease:

HCPP *[honey comb paper puff]* finial with clown and cherub, N *[novelty]*, c. 1930s, no maker *[maker of Valentine is not known]*, 8.5" x 6" x 3" *[height x width x depth]*, EX *[excellent condition]*, Kreider Collection *[name of the collection]*.

As trite as it seems, this still must be said, always keep in mind your location in the United States. Unfortunately, this does play a heavy roll when determining the market value of your Valentines. Also don't forget the pricing equation from *Valentines With Values*:

CATEGORY + CONDITION + SIZE + MANUFACTURER + ARTIST SIGNATURE + AGE + LOCATION x MULTIPLIED BY THE SQUARE ROOT OF, THE HEART = A HIGHER VALUE.

This does not imply you are to buy Valentines this way! It does reflect the reality of how many collectors purchase their Valentines. Therefore, no matter how definitive Valentine collecting becomes, the heart is still a major factor in the fluctuating market place.

Finally, please remember that this book was designed to be used. To become worn, soiled, and scarred from constant handling would be the best thing that could happen to it and will give the collector his or her best reward. With this in mind, let us move on to Chapter I.

Chapter One

♥ Novelty ♥

Novelty cards are those Valentines that are unique in style. Not a typical greeting card style, this type of card could be one that was played with, such as: cut-out paper dolls, finger puppets, fans, etc. Or, a gift might be attached to the card: for instance, some perfume, a linen hankie or a fingernail file. Novelty cards can also have a comic character or movie personality printed on them. This category of card crosses over into all of the styles of valentine cards: greeting, dimensional, flats, mechanical-flats, and postcards.

In *Valentines With Values*, I spoke about comic Valentines through the ages and focused primarily on the original comic Valentines (penny dreadfuls), and touched lightly upon the comic character, movie personality, and cartoon character Valentine cards. Now I would like to discuss the novelty Valentine card in more detail.

For years there have been satirical, one-page illustrations representing our political, social, and editorialized views of our world of the moment. As we looked at the penny dreadfuls in *Valentines With Values*, you could see from the mid-1800s on there were wonderful examples of using satire to get a smirk.

Many things seem to migrate from Europe to America, so did the comic strip. English caricaturist Thomas Rowlandson drew Dr. Syntax, who is believed to be the very first regular cartoon character, and Swiss artist and educator, Rodolphe Töpffer, created a prototype of the comic strip for his students in 1827, entitled *"histoires en estampes."*

There seems to be some disagreement on which was the very first American cartoon strip. Some people believe it was *Hogan's Alley*, which appeared on May 5, 1895, in the *New York World*, the illustrator was Richard Felton Outcault. Later in 1896, it was syndicated featuring *The Yellow Kid*, in Hearst Newspapers. There is another group of people who say the first "true" comic strip was *The Katzenjammer Kids*, illustrated by Rudolph Dirks. It appeared in 1897 in a supplement called *The American Humorist*, part of *The New York Journal*, published by W.B. Hearst. Still another group claims that *Little Bears*, illustrated by James Guilford Swinnerton, appearing in 1895 in the *San Francisco Examiner*, was the first. Whatever you choose to believe, we only know for sure that the comic strip started with one of the above mentioned characters.

Some of the most popular of the early 1900s characters were: *Buster Brown* (Outcault original), *Little Nemo in Slumberland*, illustrated by Winsor McCay; and *Foxy Grandpa*, illustrated by Charles E. Schultze.

Mr. A. Mutt or as a lot of us remember *Mutt and Jeff*, created by Bud Fisher, gets the credit for being the first successful daily comic strip. *Blondie*, created by Chic Young, also was one of the most widely syndicated comic strips of the 1930s.

Originally, the Sunday comic strips were geared more towards the youth of America. Gradually the daily strip evolved into entertainment for the adult population.

In 1914, *Abie the Agent* was introduced as the first definitive adult comic strip in the United States. This strip was designed by Harry Hershfield. Hershfield's innovative comic strip about a Jewish middle-class businessman appeared as a nationally syndicated comic strip from 1914 to 1932 and from 1935 to 1940. There were four lost years of "Abie" during a contractual dispute over the cartoonist signing his work. As in all businesses, CEOs are always looking for ways to improve their profit margins. By not having a cartoonist sign his work, his personal following was reduced and therefore so was his salary demands, according to historian Jerry Robinson.

By 1935, Hershfield worked out an agreement with Hearst, which gave the cartoonist the right to sign his work and also gave him a byline. "Abie again appeared in the *Journal*, from 1935 to 1940."

As the comic strip business became more popular, so did the various types of comic strips. At first they would just tell a short humorous story to make you laugh. As time went by there was another type of strip introduced into the main stream of the comic section: adventure strips. Included within this type of strip was a "cliff hanger," which kept the reader's attention from week to week or day to day. Two of the most popular adventure strip characters were Buck Rogers and Tarzan. *Buck Rogers* was illustrated by Richard W. Calkins and written by Philip Nowlan. *Tarzan* was first created and illustrated by Harold Foster, who also gave us *Prince Valiant*.

Another ingenious change in the comic strip was the arrival of *Gasoline Alley*, illustrated by Frank O. King, in 1919. What was different about this strip was that the characters grew older along with the population, whereas in the other strips the characters did not age. Even today, most comic strip characters do not grow old.

When it comes to ground breaking marks in the comic strip industry, we cannot forget *Dick Tracy*. This strip was the first to portray a human being shot with a gun. The year it appeared was 1931, a very realistic depiction of the times. At the other end of the spectrum, we had fantasy comic strips, such as *Flash Gordon*, created by Alex Raymond in 1934, and *Terry and the Pirates* created by Milton Caniff in 1934.

Once the comic character or movie personality became a success, ground was broken for more profitable avenues, for example, the manufacturing of items, such as greeting cards, books, games, dolls, watches, and so on. The creator of the strip would sometimes be the owner of the comic strip or character, or there would be a license agreement by the strip's newspaper syndicate that would be enforced when other merchandise was manufactured with that particular comic strip character or movie personality. Later on, some of the prime targets for this type of merchandising would be our favorite comic strip, movie, and TV personalities, heroes and heroines: Gene Autry, Roy Rogers, Dick Tracy, Dennis the Menace, Betty Boop, Minnie Mouse, James Cagney, Joe Penner, LuLu, the Wizard of Oz, etc.

Many of these characters appeared on greeting cards as you will see on the following pages. Remember that they made official copyrighted cards and unofficial knock-off cards, meaning they were drawn by artists other than the official illustrator. (A knockoff means a copy or imitation of someone or something popular.) The image would look very similar to the original image, but the artist would have to change the character's hair color or some other defining feature of that character in order to legally market that particular item. Many of the comic strips had a writer and an illustrator, just as the greeting card companies had when they designed their cards. This was not the case all of the time, for instance, J.G. Scott, is a perfect example of someone who illustrated his work as well as composed his own verses.

Walt Disney is probably the best-known cartoon artist and producer of animated films. It was not until 1928, when he introduced the world to *Steamboat Willie* and what would become his most popular cartoon character: Mickey Mouse. Disney's first feature-length cartoon films were: *Snow White and the Seven Dwarfs* in 1937, followed by *Pinocchio* in 1940, *Fantasia* in 1941, and *Bambi* in 1942. Disney controlled every aspect of his ventures, from children's books to greeting cards.

Within this chapter, you will see a variety of official Disney Valentine cards. There are various discrepancies regarding how many cards are in a particular series. Any additional information that can be added to confirm the number in a series would be appreciated, please write or call me, so this documentation can be made more definitive for the collector and dealer.

Keep in mind, as the generations change so will the fluctuation in prices for cards portraying these characters. After a while, the generations will no longer remember *Katazenjammer Kids* or *The Yellow Kid*, bringing the value of these artifacts down. Even though these items would be considered rare, unless you are an elitist in your field of collecting, you will not be interested in adding characters that do not represent a particular happy moment in your maturing years here on earth.

Characters such as Peanuts, The Lion King, Barbie, Michael Jordan, Power Rangers, Star Trek, Pink Panther, and Winnie the Pooh will go up in value, balance out, and then drop, as the transition of each new generation takes place in society. Another thing to watch are trends in the movie industry. Once in a while a company will rerelease an original motion picture, such as, *The Wizard of Oz, Pinocchio, Snow White,* etc., bringing the value back up again, due to the current popularity of the movie and the characters in the movie.

Listed on the next couple of pages are some of the most popular comic characters and their friends to help you identify the characters that may appear on the Valentine cards.

♥♥♥♥♥♥♥♥♥♥♥♥♥♥

Comic Characters and Their Friends

Batman™
Born: May, 1939
Originator: Bob Kane
Friends: Robin the Boy Wonder; Joker, Riddler, Penguin, Cat Woman.

Betty Boop™
Born: July, 1934
Originator: Max Fleischer
Friends: Koko the Clown, Bimbo the Dog.

Bonzo™
Born: 1931
Originator: George E. Studdy
Friends: None

Bringing Up Father™
Born: January, 1913
Originator: George McManus
Friends: Jiggs, Maggie, Nora (the daughter), Dinty Moore (owner of the tavern).

Buster Brown™
Born: May, 1902
Originator: Richard F. Outcault
Friends: Mary Jane, Tige his dog, Buddy Tucker.

Charlie Chaplin™
Born: 1915
Originator: there were many
Friends: Brutis, Luke the Gook.

Dennis the Menace™
Born: 1951
Originator: Hank Ketchum
Friends: Margaret, Joey, Mr. Wilson, Dennis's parents.

Dick Tracy™
Born: 1931
Originator: Chester Gould
Friends: B.O. Plenty, Sparkle Plenty, Gravel Gertie, Tess Trueheart, Pat Patton, and Bonny Braids.

Felix the Cat™
Born: 1923
Originator: Pat Sullivan, Otto Messmer
Friends: Phyllis (his girlfriend).

Flash Gordon™
Born: 1934
Originator: Alex Raymond, illustrator, and Don Moore, writer
Friends: Dr. Zarkov, Ming the Merciless, Dale Arden

The Flintstones™
Born: 1960
Originator: Hanna-Barbera Studios
Friends: Pebbles Flintstone, Wilma Flintstone, Bamm-Bamm Rubble, Baby Puss, Dino, Barney, Betty Rubble

Foxy Grandpa™
Born: 1900
Originator: Charles Edward Schultze
Friends: two boys with no name

Gasoline Alley™
Born: 1918
Originator: Frank King
Friends: Auntie Blossom, Corky, Skeezix, Judy, Doc, Bill, Nina, Uncle Avery, Uncle Walt

Happy Hooligan™
Born: 1900
Originator: Frederick Burr Opper
Friends: Lord Montmorency, Flip the dog, Gloomy Gus

Henry™
Born: 1934
Originator: Carl Anderson
Friends: Henrietta (his girlfriend)

The Katzenjammer Kids™
Born: 1897
Originator: Rudolph Dirks
Friends: Mamma, Rollo Rhubarb, Miss Twiddle, Fritz, Lena, Hans the Inspector, Captain

Kewpie™
Born: early 1900s
Originator: Rose O'Neill
Friends: none

Krazy Kat™
Born: 1910
Originator: George Herriman
Friends: Archy, Officer Pupp, Ignatz

Little LuLu™
Born: 1950
Originator: Marjorie Henderson Buell (Margo)
Friends: Tubby Tompkins, Wilbur Van Snobbe, Alvin

Little Nemo in Slumberland™
Born: 1905
Originator: Winsor McCay
Friends: King Morpheous, Doctor Pill, Flip, Impy, Nemo

Moon Mullins™
Born: 1923
Originator: Frank Willard
Friends: Lord Plushbottom, Uncle Willie, Mamie, Emmy Schmatlz, Kayo.

The Newlyweds™
Born: 1904
Originator: George McManus
Friends: Snookums, their baby

Peanuts™
Born: 1950
Originator: Charles Schulz
Friends: Lucy, Linus, Snoopy, Peppermint Patty, Pig-pen, Franklin, Schroeder

Popeye™
Born: 1929
Originator: E.C. Segar
Friends: Wimpy, Olive Oly, Jeep, Swee' Pea

Superman™
Born: 1939
Originator: Joe Shuster, illustrator, and Jerry Siegel, writer
Friends: Lois Lane, Jimmey Olsen, Perry White (Editor of the Daily Planet), Clark Kent (Superman)

Toonerville Folks™
Born: 1908
Originator: Fontaine Fox
Friends: Mickey McGuire, Little Woo-Woo Wortle, Mr. Bang, Grandma Demon Chaperone, Aunt Eppy Hogg, Skipper and his Trolley, Snake-Tongue Tompkins, Pinckney Wortle, Katrinka, and Uncle Chew Wilson

Wonder Woman™
Born: 1944
Originator: H.G. Peter, illustrator, and Charles Moulton, writer
Friends: Capt. Steve Trevor, Diana Prince (Wonder Woman)

The Yellow Kid™
Born: 1895
Originator: Richard F. Outcault
Friends: None

Yogi Bear™
Born: 1958
Originator: Hanna-Barbera Studios
Friends: Boo Boo, Ranger Smith, Cindy (his girl friend), Snagglepuss, Fibber Fox, Yakky Doodle, Chopper the Bulldog, Alfy Gator

A pair of "paper doll" or "dressed" Valentines, handmade, c. 1910, German, their faces are made of Victorian scraps and their outfits were carefully made of silk. Note: the young lady is holding a Valentine card, they are surrounded with dried plants, including edelweiss from the high Alps, they are both framed, another example of a "Paper Doll" valentine can be found on page 130 in *Valentines With Values* (in *Valentines With Values* the terminology is not correct on p. 130. It should have said "Dressed"). The actual Valentine without the frame measures 6" x 4.25". This type of Valentine is highly sought after by most collectors, rare, hand written at the top of each card is: "*Gruss Aus,*" meaning "Greetings From," NM, Kreider Collection.

Good	Excellent	Near Mint
$30.00	$175.00(each)	$275.00(each)

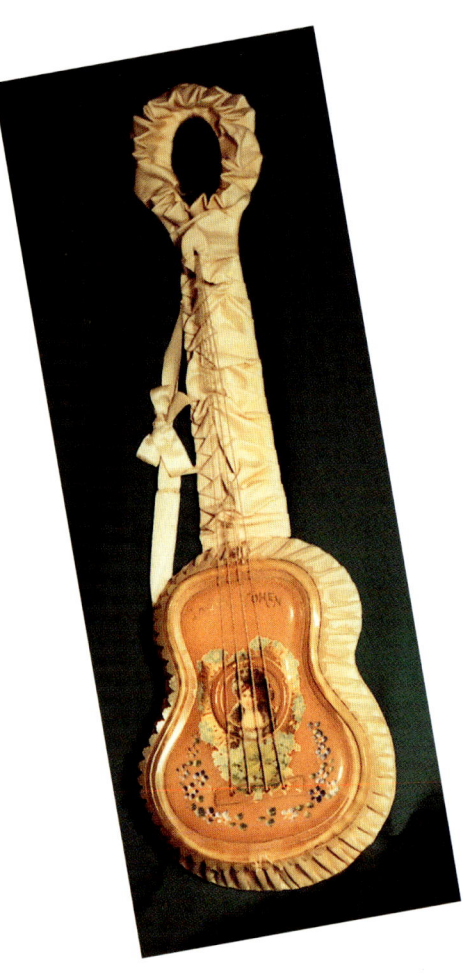

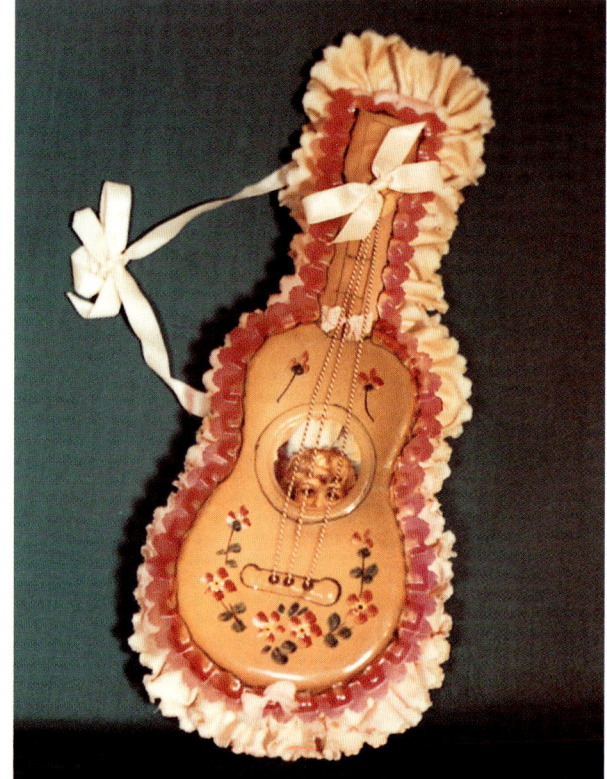

Guitar made of celluloid with original polished cotton pleated around the base, face of guitar is hand painted with the words, "Love's Token", original ribbon made of silk-satin, original strings made of cord attached with metal rivets, N, c. early 1900s, no maker, 22" x 6.5" x 2", EX, Kreider Collection.

Good	Excellent	Near Mint
$50.00	$800.00	$1200.00

Guitar made of celluloid with orignial polished cotton ruffle around the base of guitar, corrugated paper around the depth, hand painted on face with Victorian scrap of little girl inside and original silk-satin ribbon used on handle of guitar and hanging ribbon, strings of guitar are made of cord attached with metal rivets, N, c. early 1900s, no maker, 11" x 5" x 1", NM, Kreider Collection.

Good	Excellent	Near Mint
$15.00	$150.00	$250.00

Heart-shaped guitar made of pyroxylin with original ruffled polished cotton bordering guitar, original silk-satin ribbon for hanging and bows, image on face of guitar is a Victorian scrap attached with metal rivets underneath the face of the guitar, original strings made of cord attached with rivets, also shown opened with a black and white photo added, N, if you know the difference between pyroxylin and celluliod this will help date your artifact more accurately, you can see the difference with the visible eye, see page 129 in *Valentines With Values,* for another example of a pyroxylin piece, c. early 1900s, 10" x 4.5" x 1", EX, Kreider Collection.

Good	Excellent	Near Mint
$30.00	$150.00	$300.00

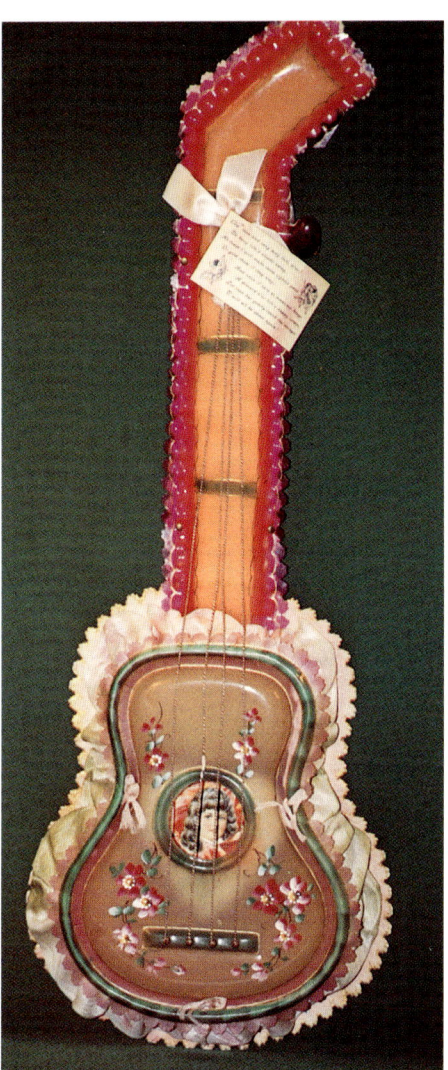

Guitar made of celluloid, with original ruffled polished cotton bordering guitar, original silk-satin ribbon on handle of guitar, face is hand painted, original acquaintance card attached, c. early 1900s, 21.75" x 8" x 2", NM, Herstad Collection.

Good	Excellent	Near Mint
$50.00	$800.00	$1200.00

Banjo made of pyroxylin, bordered with ruffled polished cotton, inside of banjo is a chromolitho picture of two children pasted on the back and a Victorian cherub attached with a wire to give it a dimensional look, all ribbon and cording original. Note: the unusual ecru color, N, c. early 1900s, 10" x 5" x 1", G, Kreider Collection.

Good	Excellent	Near Mint
$30.00	$150.00	$300.00

HCPP hanging heart, NM, c. 1920s, arrows are movable, made in U.S.A., size shown: 8" x 8" x 3.5", also comes in a smaller size, EX, Kreider Collection.

Good	Excellent	Near Mint
$5.00	$75.00	$125.00

HCPP clown, front, back, opened and closed, N, c. 1920s, no maker, 6.75" x 6" x 2" when opened showing the HCPP clown, NM, very unusual, Kreider Collection.

Good	Excellent	Near Mint
$5.00	$50.00	$75.00

Pedestal HCPP with children playing in the snow, N, c. 1930s, made in U.S.A., 8.5" x 6.5" x 3.25", EX, Kreider Collection.

Good	Excellent	Near Mint
$2.00	$35.00	$50.00

HCPP basket with hearts, N, c. 1920s, USA, made by: Beistle Co., Shippensburg, Pa, patents July 14, 1925, and July 27, 1926 (another version is pictured on page 146 in *Valentines With Values*), 10" x 7" x 6", EX, Kreider Collection.

Good	Excellent	Near Mint
$5.00	$75.00	$125.00

HCPP finial with clown and cherub, N, c. 1930s, no maker, 8.5" x 6" x 3", EX, Kreider Collection.

Good	Excellent	Near Mint
$3.00	$35.00	$50.00

Wheel of Love, top and base made of HCPP, NM, c. 1920s, made by Beistle Co., Shippensburg, Pa. (another version is pictured on page 146 in *Valentines With Values*), another card for all of the "wheel watchers" out there, 9.5" x 6.5" x 3", EX, Kreider Collection.

Good	Excellent	Near Mint
$2.00	$75.00	$125.00

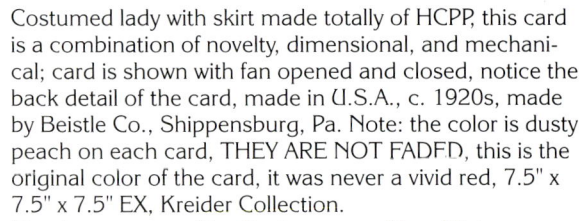

Costumed lady with skirt made totally of HCPP, this card is a combination of novelty, dimensional, and mechanical; card is shown with fan opened and closed, notice the back detail of the card, made in U.S.A., c. 1920s, made by Beistle Co., Shippensburg, Pa. Note: the color is dusty peach on each card, THEY ARE NOT FADED, this is the original color of the card, it was never a vivid red, 7.5" x 7.5" x 7.5" EX, Kreider Collection.

Good	Excellent	Near Mint
$5.00	$75.00	$125.00

Dan Cupid teaching students about LOVE, the card also is a combination of novelty, dimensional, and mechanical, opens like a fan, c. 1930s, made in U.S.Am., 6.5" x 8" x 2", EX, Kreider Collection.

Good	Excellent	Near Mint
$2.00	$25.00	$35.00

HCPP heart as center motif with base made up of HCPP and Victorian scrap of child attached to base, N, c.1930s, no maker, 4" x 3.5" x 1.5", EX, Kreider Collection.

Good	Excellent	Near Mint
$1.00	$5.00	$10.00

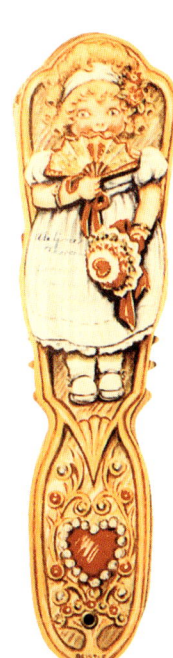

Fan made of HCPP, NM, c. early 1920s, made by Beistle Co., Shippensburg, Pa. Shown front, opened and back, printed in U.S.A., 8.5" high x 2" wide when closed, opened fan measures approximately 7", NM, Kreider Collection.

Good	Excellent	Near Mint
$5.00	$95.00	$150.00

Fan, N, with original tassel, sold for 50 cents, c. late 1950s-early 1960s, made by Hallmark, 8.5" high x 7.5" wide, NM, Campbell Collection.

Good	Excellent	Near Mint
$1.00	$5.00	$10.00

Miniature hand held fan, NF, chromolitho, c. early 1900s, no maker, 4.5" x 3", NM, Kreider Collection.

Good	Excellent	Near Mint
$ 2.00	$25.00	$35.00

Heart-shaped cards in original box with cast metal skate and football player attached to cards, N, c. 1920s-1930s, made in U.S.A., no maker, see page 141 in *Valentines With Values*, for two other cards in this series without the original boxes, how many in this series are unknown at this time, cards measure without box: 5.5" x 5.25", M, Honberger Collection.

Good	Excellent	Near Mint
$15.00	$50.00	$75.00

Gift-giving, NGC, still filled with original red hot hearts, c. 1950s, made by Barker Cards, copyright Baker, Cincinnati, U.S.A., "Cards to Remember," sold for 15 cents (for an example of Valentine with original candy see page 144 in: *Valentines With Values*), 7.5" x 3.75, NM, Kreider Collection.

Good	Excellent	Near Mint
$2.00	$15.00	$25.00

Charlie McCarthy, Boston Bull, Pekingese, and lady on wagon, lollipop gift-giving cards, N, all manufactured by Rosen Company, Providence, R.I. All came with a lollipop. Note: Charlie McCarthy is rare, this card opens up and comes with six lollipops, the value of this card is definitely higher than the others, c. late 1930s, McCarthy card measures 8.5" x 5.75", the other cards came in two sizes, 6" x 5" and 3.5" x 3.25", see pages 144 and 145 for other images used on these cards in *Valentines With Values*, EX, McCarthy card: Herstad Collection and other cards from: Kreider Collection.

Charlie McCarthy value:

Good	Excellent	Near Mint
$10.00	$75.00	$125.00

Other cards approximate value:

Good	Excellent	Near Mint
$2.00	$15.00	$25.00

Elephant spraying water and girl playing baseball, lollipop gift-giving cards, N, c. 1940s, no maker, made in U.S.A., Elephant measures: 4" x 5", baseball girl measures: 5" x 3.75", any card with a sports related theme commands a higher value, EX, Kreider Collection.

Good	Excellent	Near Mint
$1.00	$10.00	$15.00

Pocket knife shown closed and opened, NMF, c. 1940s, made in U.S.A., opened knife measures 4" x 5", see page 147 in *Valentines With Values,* for another pocket knife version, NM, Kreider Collection.

Good	Excellent	Near Mint
$3.00	$15.00	$25.00

"My Heart Beats for You," N, clock-work, heart beats up and down when wound, No. 529, how many in this series are still unknown, made by: H. Fishlove & Co., made in Chicago, IL, made for Coopers, Kenosha, Wis.(for another in this series see page 139 in *Valentines With Values*), 5.5" x 4", NM, Kreider Collection.

Good	Excellent	Near Mint
$5.00	$50.00	$75.00

Couple kissing on the dance floor, NF with D, arm is placed on a spring, licensed under Gergroy Patents, initials printed on bottom right hand corner, *LCH*, 7" x 5", Kreider Collection.

Good	Excellent	Near Mint
$ 5.00	$25.00	$45.00

Pig finger puppet, N, shown back with instructions for use, c. 1950s, no maker, original moving plastic eyes, 6.5" x 3.25", NM, Kreider Collection.

Good	Excellent	Near Mint
$3.00	$15.00	$25.00

Boy with cat, NM, boy has original plastic eyes, c. 1930s, PIG, with side easel, 9.5" x 5.75", NM, Kreider Collection.

Good	Excellent	Near Mint
$3.00	$25.00	$35.00

Butterscotch tiger cat, NF, with easel back, original plastic eyes, c. 1940s, no maker, 3.75" x 3", EX, Kreider Collection.
Good	Excellent	Near Mint
$2.00	$5.00	$10.00

School boy with original plastic eyes, N booklet, has story inside, c. 1940s, no maker, made in U.S.A., 6" x 3.5", NM, Kreider Collection.
Good	Excellent	Near Mint
$2.00	15.00	$25.00

Farmer with black glass eyes, NMF, c. early 1900s, made by: Raphael Tuck & Sons, PIG, unusual card for Tuck, 7" x 4.25", EX, Kreider Collection.
Good	Excellent	Near Mint
$5.00	$25.00	$45.00

Girlfriends trading hearts, with original plastic eyes, NMF, with easel back, c. early 1920s, PIG, 8.5" x 5.5", NM, Kreider Collection.
Good	Excellent	Near Mint
$5.00	$25.00	$35.00

"Love-O-Grams" shown closed and open with dimensional pop-up figures, all signed by Charles Twelvetrees, U.S. Pat. No. 2102.553, how many in this series are unknown at this time, c. 1920s-1930s, another version in this series is shown on page 135 in *Valentines With Values*, 4.5" high, opens to 13", EX, Kreider Collection.

Good	Excellent	Near Mint
$5.00	$50.00	$75.00

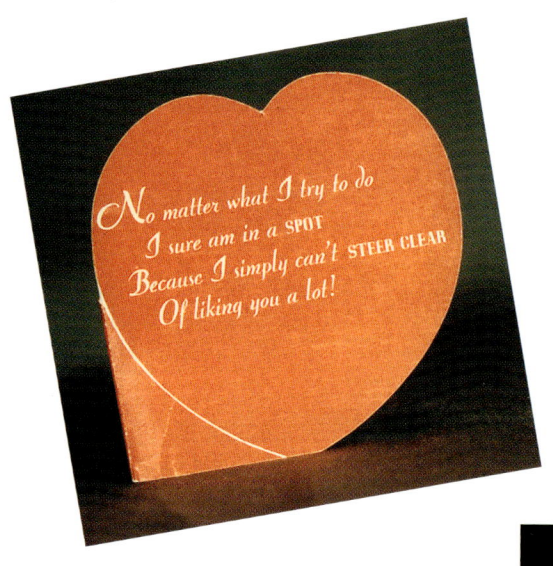

Scenic and transportation images, NGC, shown opened and closed, c. 1920s-1930s, all signed by Charles Twelvetrees, how many in this series are still unknown, 4.5" x 9", EX, Kreider Collection.

Good	Excellent	Near Mint
$5.00	$50.00	$75.00

Paper doll Valentine, NGC, with original pieces, c. 1930s, no maker imprinted on card, possibly Whitney made, 5" x 5", EX, Kreider Collection.

Good	Excellent	Near Mint
$5.00	$35.00	$45.00

Paper doll cards, NF, c. 1930s, made by A-MERI-CARD, made in U.S.A., how many in this series are still unknown. Nos. on back of each card: P150, 137, 69441, all measure: 4.5" x 5", M, Kreider Collection.

Good	Excellent	Near Mint
$5.00	$35.00	$45.00

Valentine cut-out doll booklet, NGC, c. 1950s, made in U.S.A., made by: Ameri Card, 7" x 5.5", NM, Smith Collection.

Good	Excellent	Near Mint
$5.00	$35.00	$50.00

Paper doll-type seesaw, ND, c. 1930s, probably came together on one page, has letters that you must match up when putting together, no maker, 7" long saw, 4.5" high, EX, Kreider Collection.

Good	Excellent	Near Mint
$5.00	$25.00	$45.00

Candy advertisng Valentine cards in original box, never opened, free 35-cent coupon inside for one Baby Ruth or Butterfinger, also you can win a $20,000 college Scholoarship, N, ©1985 East Hanover, NJ, Grand Award, Nashua, NH, made in U.S.A., box measures: 9.5" x 6.5" and each card measures: 4.5" x 3", M, Kreider Collection.
Values are for individual cards only:

Good	Excellent	Near Mint
$5.00	$10.00	$15.00

Alpine White Chocolate and Chunky gift-giving cards, NGC, made by American Greetings, © Nestlé's Foods Corporation 1991. Chunky is a licensed trademark of Nestlé's Foods Corporation, shown inside of both cards with a free (up to 40-cent value) coupon, both coupons expired, December 31, 1993, cards sold for $1.65, 8.25" x 5", M, Kreider Collection.
No value available at this time; cards sold for $1.65 each.

Avon scratch off Valentine cards and a hidden message will be revealed, c. 1970s, in original wrapper, comes in three-set of fun designs, manufactured by: Avon, © Avon-all rights reserved, made in U.S.A., 4" x 4", M, Donated to the Kreider Collection by Richard and Beverly Pardini, Stockton, California.
Values are for individual cards only:

Good	Excellent	Near Mint
$1.00	$5.00	$10.00

Oh Boy!, gum card, NF, with original wrapper, art deco period, made by The Buzza Co., Craftacres, Mpls., U.S.A., ©1925. Note: Oh Boy! is printed on the card, the value of this card is higher when the gum matches the card. Also notice the black lady image on this card; gum cards are very hard to find despite what some collectors might say, especially a card with the above combination on one card: gum, black, and art deco period, 7" x 4.25", EX, Kreider Collection.

Good	Excellent	Near Mint
$10.00	$125.00	$250.00

Black boy with original stick of Spearmint Gum, for other gum cards see page 133 in *Valentines With Values,* c. 1920s, 5" x 4", EX, Kreider Collection.

Good	Excellent	Near Mint
$5.00	$125.00	$250.00

Chiclets chewing gum card with original box still attached, NGC, possibly illustrated by J.G. Scott, c. 1950s, made by Gibson Card Co., 6" x 5.5". EX, Smith Collection.

Good	Excellent	Near Mint
$5.00	$75.00	$175.00

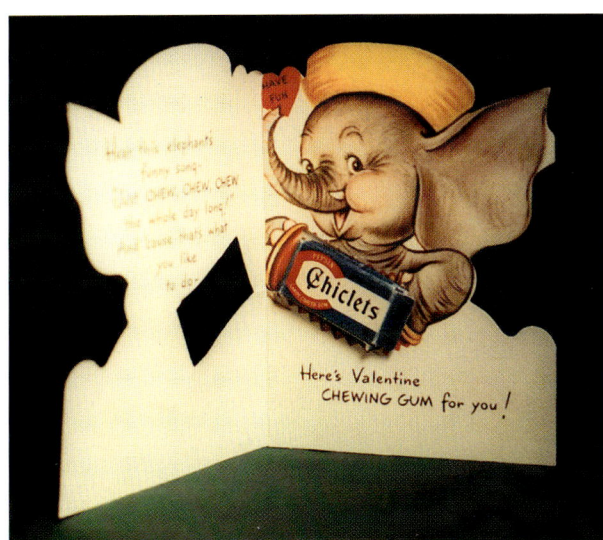

Puzzle Valentine card, N, c. 1930s-1940s, no maker, 5.5" x 5.5", NM, Kreider Collection.

Good	Excellent	Near Mint
$2.00	$25.00	$50.00

"I'd like to be your Valentine?" inside card states "My wife won't let me!" NGC, c. 1920s-1930s, made by Rust Craft, 240A, 3" x 4", NM, Kreider Collection.

Good	Excellent	Near Mint
$3.00	$15.00	$25.00

Real hair Valentine card, N, PIG, c. 1930s, with easel back, for other versions of hair on cards see page 139 in *Valentines With Values*, 6.5" x 4", NM, Smith Collection.

Good	Excellent	Near Mint
$5.00	$25.00	$50.00

Lux soap, NF, c.1930s-1940s, made in U.S.A. Note: advertising category, 3.5" x 3", NM, Kreider Collection.

Good	Excellent	Near Mint
$5.00	$30.00	$50.00

Bon "AMI", NF, c. 1950s, made in U.S.A., 3.75" x 3", NM, Kreider Collection.

Good	Excellent	Near Mint
$5.00	$25.00	$50.00

Duz, NF, c. 1950s, made in U.S.A., 3.75" x 3", NM, Kreider Collection.

Good	Excellent	Near Mint
$5.00	$25.00	$50.00

Frigid-Aire, NF, c.1950s, made in U.S.A., 3.75" x 2.75", NM, Kreider Collection.

Good	Excellent	Near Mint
$5.00	$25.00	$50.00

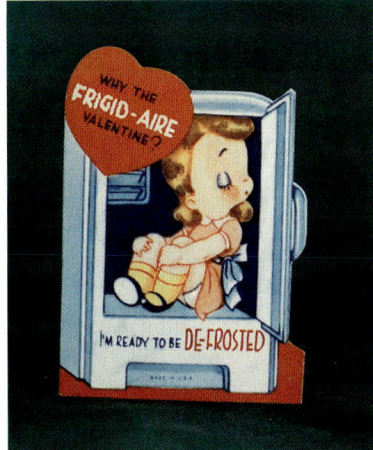

All novelty greeting cards, every day items from vegetables to rolling pins, NGC, made in U.S.A., all measure approximately 3.5" x 4", others in this pictured on pages 172 and 173 in *Valentines With Values*, how many in this series are still unknown, EX, Kreider Collection.

Good	Excellent	Near Mint
$1.00	$5.00	$10.00

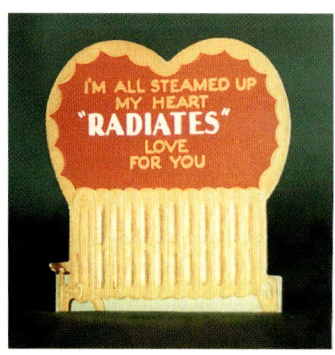

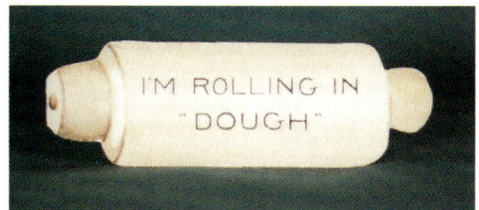

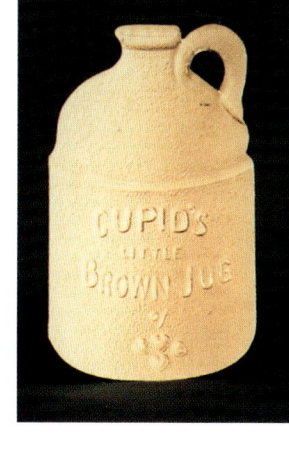

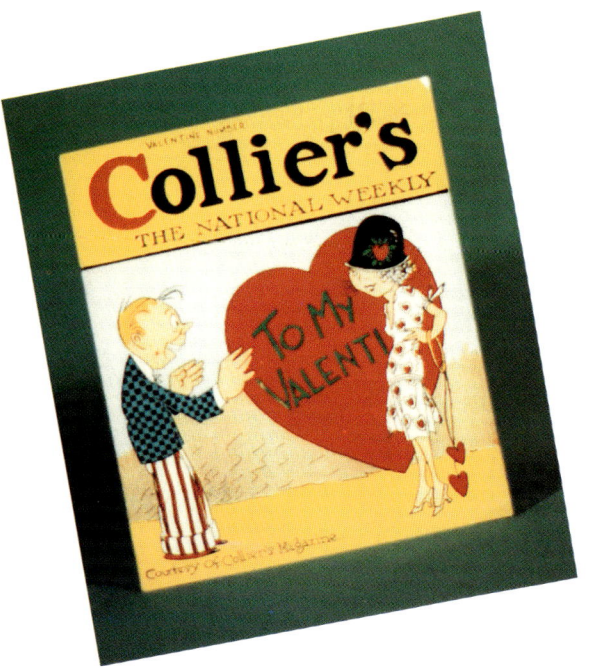

Collier's and *Ballyhoo* miniature magazine Valentines, NGC, imprinted on the front of card: Courtesy of *Ballyhoo Magazine* and Courtesy of *Collier's Magazine*, c. 1920s, made in U.S.A., 4.75" x 4", how many in this series are still unknown, EX, Kreider Collection.

Good	Excellent	Near Mint
$5.00	$25.00	$50.00

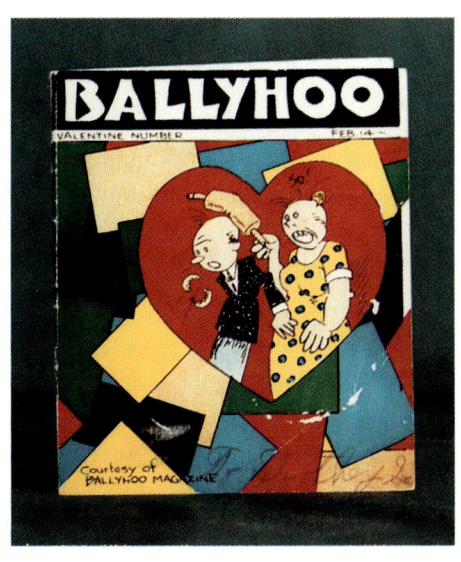

Morton Salt Girl, caricature, NF, c. 1940s, made in U.S.A., 4.5" x 3", NM, Kreider Collection.

Good	Excellent	Near Mint
$2.00	$10.00	$15.00

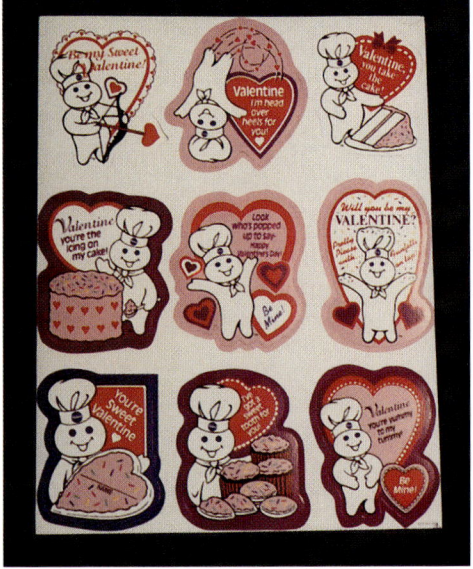

Pillsbury Dough Boy sheet of Valentines, NF, total 9 cards per sheet, M, sheet measures: 12.25" x 9.75", M, Kreider Collection. Value per individual card:

Good	Excellent	Near Mint
$3.00	$5.00	$10.00

Camel Cigarettes, NF, no maker, c. 1930s, (this card also comes with Chesterfield on it, pictured on page 172 in *Valentines With Values*), how many in this series still are unknown, 4.5" x 6.5", EX, Kreider Collection.

Good	Excellent	Near Mint
$25.00	$75.00	$125.00

Grandpa Foxy and two unknown children, NMF, chromolitho die cut, c. early 1900s, made by: *Raphael Tuck and Sons*, 10" x 9", NM, *Herstad Collection*.

Good	Excellent	Near Mint
$25.00	$150.00	$250.00

Moon Mullins caricature, shown with film strip closed and opened, NMF, c. 1920s, 4" x 5", NM, Kreider Collection.

Good	Excellent	Near Mint
$3.00	$25.00	$50.00

Cigarette and matches, NF, made by A-MERI-CARD, made in U.S.A., #108, this card is definitely politically incorrect today, 4" x 4.75", EX, Kreider Collection.

Good	Excellent	Near Mint
$5.00	$25.00	$45.00

Felix, NMF, c. 1920s. Note: there are two versions of Felix, 5" X 5", Germany (see page 103 of *One Hundred Years of Valentines* for Ignatz Mouse from Krazy Kat), EX, Herstad Collection.

Good	Excellent	Near Mint
$5.00	$50.00	$75.00

Lil' Abner, NF, made in U.S.A., c. 1940s, 6" x 5.5", EX, Herstad Collection.

Good	Excellent	Near Mint
$5.00	$50.00	$75.00

Little LuLu, ND, c. 1940s, made in U.S.A., these cards are very difficult to find, both cards were illustrated by Marjorie Henderson Buell, printed on the bottom of each card, the original illustrator of LuLu, third card pictured does not have Marjorie's name on it. It really is a caricature of LuLu instead of the original illustration as Marjorie drew her, cards measure approximately: 5" x 3.5" x 2", NM, Smith Collection, Kreider Collection and Herstad Collection.

Good	Excellent	Near Mint
$5.00	$50.00	$75.00

Popeye, NGC, official illustration, made by King Features, c. 1929, made in U.S.A. (see pages 114 and 116 in *Valentines With Values*, for other Popeye cards), 5" x 3", NM, Herstad Collection.

Good	Excellent	Near Mint
$5.00	$50.00	$75.00

Jiggs, comic character, NF, c. 1930s, made in U.S.A., has side tab (see page 114 in *Valentines With Values*, for another Valentine card with Jiggs), 5.5" x 4.5", EX, Herstad Collection.

Good	Excellent	Near Mint
$5.00	$50.00	$75.00

"Snookums" caricature from, *The Newlyweds*, NF, c. early 1900s, he is identified with having one tooth, bulb head, and moronic expression, he had a face only a mother could love, he also had the characteristic of throwing tantrums, 4.5" x 5.25", Kreider Collection.

Good	Excellent	Near Mint
$ 5.00	$50.00	$75.00

Andy Gump playing with the radio, NF, artist signed: *Sidney Smith,* c. 1930s, 4" x 5.25", NM, Herstad Collection.

Good	Excellent	Near Mint
$10.00	$75.00	$95.00

Actor James Cagney, NF, c. 1930s, made in U.S.A., very hard to find card, 5.75" x 3.5", NM, Herstad Collection.

Good	Excellent	Near Mint
$10.00	$75.00	$125.00

Rudy Vallee caricature, NFF, c. 1930s, radio and movie star, 5.75" x 5.5", if folded, .5" deep, Herstad Collection.

Good	Excellent	Near Mint
$10.00	$75.00	$95.00

Radio star, Joe Penner, NMF, c. 1930s, "I'LL gladly buy a duck," 7" high, x 4.25" wide, NM, Herstad Collection.

Good	Excellent	Near Mint
$15.00	$75.00	$125.00

Jimmy Durante caricature, NMF, made in U.S.A., c. 1940s, 11" x 6", NM, Kreider Collection.

Good	Excellent	Near Mint
$15.00	$75.00	$125.00

Wonder Woman, NF, c. 1940s, made in U.S.A., Wonder Woman is a very difficult card to find, 6" x 6", NM, Herstad Collection.

Good	Excellent	Near Mint
$15.00	$75.00	$150.00

Superman, official version, ©1940s, Superman, Inc., made in U.S.A., both cards measure 4.5" x 6.5", EX, Herstad Collection.

Good	Excellent	Near Mint
$10.00	$75.00	$125.00

Dick Tracy, NFF, c. 1940s, made in U.S.A., also a difficult card to find, 6" x 5.5", EX, Herstad Collection.

Good	Excellent	Near Mint
$15.00	$75.00	$150.00

Mickey and Minnie, unofficial version, N, c. 1930s, 5" x 3.75", EX, Herstad Collection.

Good	Excellent	Near Mint
$5.00	$25.00	$35.00

Mickey and Minnie Mouse, NGC, official version, c. 1930s, *Walt Disney Enterprise*, published by Hall Bros. 4.5" x 3.5", EX, very difficult to find, Herstad Collection.

Good	Excellent	Near Mint
$10.00	$50.00	$75.00

Flocked rabbit, NF, with side easels, c. late 1940s, Hallmark, copyrighted by Hall Bros., this card sold for 25 cents (see page 170 in *Valentines With Values* for other flocked and felt-eared cards), made in U.S.A, 8.5" x 7". Note: revised price, EX, Kreider Collection.

Good	Excellent	Near Mint
$2.00	$10.00	$15.00

Fireman with original rubber hose, NF, easel back, c. 1940s, made in Chicago, IL, by Carrington Co. (see page 136 in *Valentines With Values*) for two other cards in this rubber hose series, 8" x 5", NM, Kreider Collection.

Good	Excellent	Near Mint
$5.00	$35.00	$45.00

Tennis player, NF, c. 1950s, Litho, U.S.A., Note: see page 142 in: *Valentines With Values*, for the Fuller Brush advertising version, 5" x 2", EX, Kreider Collection.

Good	Excellent	Near Mint
50 cents	$3.00	$5.00

Punch-out cards, NF, c. 1950s, no maker, all different sizes and categories, how many in this series are still unknown, EX, Kreider Collection.

Good	Excellent	Near MInt
$1.00	$3.00	$5.00

Con-G-nial, Re-a-Range, and W-One-Der, NF, c. 1940s, how many in this series are still unknown, no maker, all measure 4" x 4", EX, Kreider Collection.

Good	Excellent	Near Mint
$2.00	$10.00	$15.00

K-ater to me, NF, c. 1940s, no maker, 4.25" x 2.75", EX, Kreider Collection.
Good	Excellent	Near Mint
$2.00	$10.00	$15.00

B-e Yourself, C-ee How Much, NF, c. 1940s, back of card is showing publisher printed on the back: Carrington Co., Chicago, IL (how many in this series are unknown at this time), 3.75" x 2.5", NM, Kreider Collection.
Good	Excellent	Near Mint
$2.00	$10.00	$15.00

A Loaf-er, shown closed and open, NGC, c. 1940s, made in U.S.A., 3" x 4", EX, Kreider Collection.
Good	Excellent	Near Mint
$1.00	$5.00	$10.00

Miniature flower greeting cards with little girls hidden among the petals inside each card, c. 1930s, how many in series are unknown, all measure approximately 2" x 3", EX, Kreider Collection.

Good	Excellent	Near Mint
$2.00	$5.00	$10.00

Miniature flower greeting cards with little children on the front of each card as center focus, c. 1930s, all measure approximately 3" x 2.5", EX, Kreider Collection.

Good	Excellent	Near Mint
$1.00	$5.00	$10.00

Miniature flower greeting card version to be put together as actual standing flower, stem is made out of a pipe cleaner, c. 1930s, came in a kit form and was put together by a school child, stands 4" x 2" and 3" deep, EX, Kreider Collection.

Good	Excellent	Near Mint
$2.00	$5.00	$10.00

Vegetable children, NGC, c. 1940s, made in U.SA., how many vegetable children in this series are still unknown, all measure approximately 3" x 3", EX, Kreider Collection.
Good	Excellent	Near Mint
$1.00	$5.00	$10.00

Egyptian Sphinx, NF, with dimensional effect, c. 1940s, no maker, 5.5" x 3.25", EX, Kreider Collection.
Good	Excellent	Near Mint
1.00	$5.00	$10.00

Cub Scout and Brownie card, NF, c. 1950s-1960s made in U.S.A., 6.25" x 3.25", EX, Kreider Collection.
Good	Excellent	Near MInt
$3.00	$15.00	$25.00

All 1960s with a wonderful 3 dimensional effect on each card. Please look carefully, they truly are representative of the 1960s, i.e., hair, ear muffs, ribbon, boa, macrame belt, macrame cuffs, bunny's tail, macrame daisy, yarn bow, a great example of a series of cards, how many in this series are still unknown, NF, all made in U.S.A., 4.25" x 2.75" or 5.75" x 2.5", NM, Kreider Collection.

Good	Excellent	Near Mint
$1.00	$5.00	$10.00

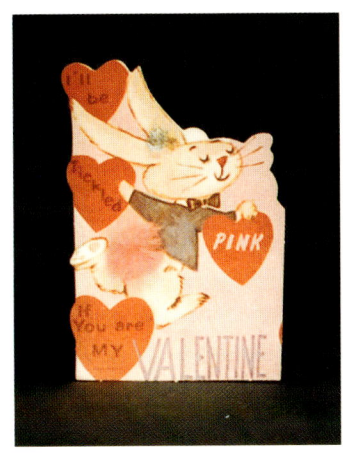

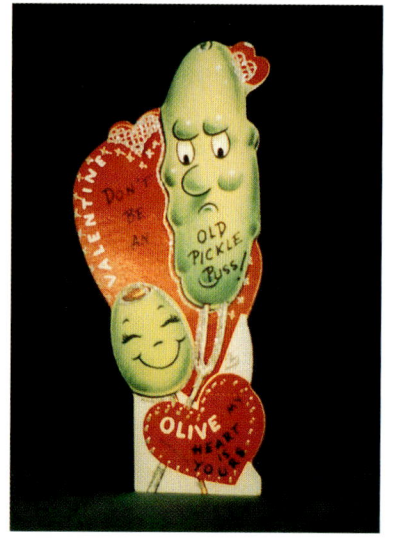

All 1960 glitter cards, NF, made in U.S.A., they represent all sorts of great categories from mushrooms to atomizers, all measure approximately 4.75" x 2", NM, Kreider Collection.

Good	Excellent	Near Mint
$1.00	$5.00	$10.00

Cinderella's Prince Charming caricature, NF, c. 1950s, 5.75" x 3", NM, Kreider Collection.

Good	Excellent	Near Mint
$2.00	$10.00	$15.00

Little Red Riding Hood, NF, c. 1950s, made in 5.5" x 2.5", EX, Kreider Collection.

Good	Excellent	Near Mint
$3.00	$25.00	$50.00

Little Red Riding Hood and the Big Bad Wolf, NF, c. 1950s, made in U.S.A., 4.75" x 6.5", EX, Kreider Collection.

Good	Excellent	Near Mint
$3.00	$25.00	$50.00

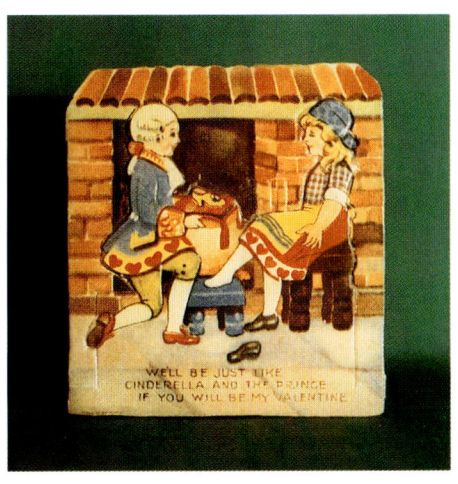

Cinderella, Hansel and Gretel, Jack Horner, and The Three Bears, NF, with easel back, MIG, c. 1920s, all are varied sizes, approximately 4.5" x 3.25", how many in this series are still unknown, EX, Kreider Collection.

Good	Excellent	Near Mint
$2.00	$15.00	$25.00

Jack in the Beanstalk, Pied Piper, Puss n' Boots and Miss Muffet, NGC booklet, c. 1940s, made in U.S.A., also included in this series are: Cinderella, Jack Horner, Little Bo Peep (all pictured on pages 122-124 in *Valentines With Values*, how many are in series are still unknown, all have original ribbons, all measure: 6.5" x 3.5", EX, Kreider Collection.

Good	Excellent	Near Mint
$5.00	$25.00	$35.00

Rapunzal, NF, with HCPP as terrace, PIG, c. 1940s, no maker, 6.5" x 5", EX, Kreider Collection.

Good	Excellent	Near Mint
$3.00	$15.00	$25.00

Three blind mice, NF, c. 1940s, made in U.S.A., 5" x 4", EX, Kreider Collection.

Good	Excellent	Near Mint
$3.00	$15.00	$25.00

Tinman and Cowardly lion caricatures, NF, c. 1960s, made in U.S.A., two sizes pictured: 5" x 4" and 4" x 2.75", Kreider Collection.

Good	Excellent	Near Mint
$3.00	$15.00	$25.00

Wizard of Oz, official version, NF, c. 1930s, licensed by Loew's, Inc. from motion picture, *Wizard of Oz*, how many in this series are still unknown, 4.5" x 6.5", EX, Herstad Collection.

Good	Excellent	Near Mint
$5.00	$75.00	$125.00

Glinda the good witch, official version, NF, back of card shows the offical logo: Loew's Incorporated, from Motion Picture, Wizard of Oz, how many in this series are still unknown, 5" x 3", EX, Kreider Collection.

Good	Excellent	Near Mint
$5.00	$25.00	$50.00

Wizard of Oz Valentine cards in original box, c. 1988, offical ©1939 Loew's Inc., Ren. 1965 MGM, Inc., ©1988 Turner Ent. Co., all rights reserved, published by Turner division of Gibson Greetings, Inc., M, Kreider Collection.
Cards value as individual cards:

Good	Excellent	Near Mint
$5.00	$10.00	$15.00

The Big Bad Wolf and the Three Pigs, NF, 1950s, made in U.S.A. (another version of the bad wolf and three pigs are pictured on pages 124 and 125 in *Valentines With Values*), opened the card measures: 8.5" x 3", EX, Kreider Collection.

Good	Excellent	Near Mint
$5.00	$35.00	$45.00

Alice in Wonderland, NF, c. 1940s, made in U.S.A., apparently there are only 5 cards in this series, these cards are very difficult to find, both cards measure approximately 5.25" x 6.5", EX, Herstad Collection.

Good	Excellent	Near Mint
$15.00	$75.00	$150.00

Ella Cinders, comic character, NF, she is sometimes mistaken for Betty Boop, c. 1930, original illustrator was Charlie Plumb, 6" x 4.5", EX, Kreider Colletion.

Good	Excellent	Near Mint
$5.00	$50.00	$75.00

Peter, Peter, Pumpkin Eater, NF, c. 1940s, no maker (another version is pictured on page 125 in *Valentines With Values*), 4" x 3.25", EX, Kreider Collection.

Good	Excellent	Near Mint
$3.00	$15.00	$25.00

Mary Had a Little Lamb, NF, c. 1950s, manufactured by Carrington Co., Chicago, Ill. (other cards with Mary are pictured on pages 122 and 123 in *Valentines With Values*), 3" x 5.25", EX, Kreider Collection.

Good	Excellent	Near Mint
$3.00	$15.00	$25.00

Raggedy Ann and Andy, caricature, NF, accented with flocking on heart and tie, no maker, 4.5" x 5", NM, Kreider Collection.

Good	Excellent	Near Mint
$1.00	$5.00	$10.00

Stuffed dolls, punch-out, NF, c. 1950s, no maker, 3" x 8", EX, Kreider Collection.

Good	Excellent	Near Mint
50 cents	$3.00	$5.00

Mouseketeers, NF, c. 1950s, made in U.S.A, unofficial version, 4" x 2", EX, Kreder Collection.

Good	Excellent	Near Mint
$1.00	$5.00	$10.00

Margaret caricature from *Dennis the Menace*, NF, no maker, 5" x 3.25", NM, Kreider Collection.

Good	Excellent	Near Mint
$2.00	$15.00	$25.00

Winnie-the-Pooh, NF, official version, c. 1960s, made by Walt Disney Productions, made in U.S.A., 5.5" x 2.75", EX, Kreider Collection.

Good	Excellent	Near Mint
$5.00	$15.00	$25.00

Snow White and the Seven Dwarfs heart-shaped cards, NMF, ©1938, W.D.Ent., made in U.SA. (see page 114 in *Valentines With Values* for other in series), how many in this series are still unknown, 5.25" x 5", NM, Herstad Collection.

Good	Excellent	Near Mint
$5.00	$50.00	$75.00

Snow White and Seven Dwarfs diorama series, ©1938, Walt Disney Enterprises, made in U.SA.(cards shown with door closed and opened in *Valentines With Values*. Note: in the version pictured on page 114 in *Valentines With Values*, Dopey should be attached, see above picture, Herstad Collection), 4.75" x 7" x 1", how many in this series are still unknown, Kreider Collection.

Good	Excellent	Near Mint
$15.00	$75.00	$125.00

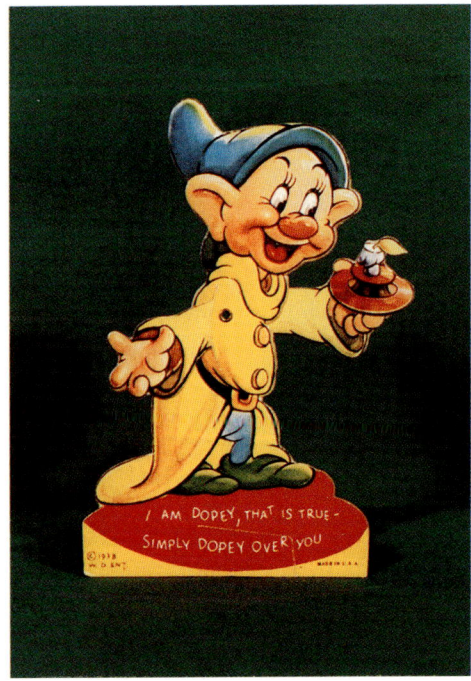

Snow White and the Seven Dwarfs, all NMF, complete set, c. 1930s, made in U.S.A., ©W.D.Ent., Snow White measures: 5.75" x 3", Dwarfs measure approximately: 5" x 2.5", NM, Kreider Collection.

Snow White:
Good	Excellent	Near Mint
$25.00	$75.00	$95.00

Individual Dwarfs:
Good	Excellent	Near Mint
$10.00	$50.00	$75.00

Clarabell, Cleo, Gideon, Goofy, Pluto, Jiminy Cricket, Minnie Mouse, Mickey Mouse, Geppetto, and Pinocchio, NMF, ©1938, W.D. Ent. made in U.S.A. (others in series pictured in *Valentines With Values* on pages 112 & 113), how many in this series are still unknown, all measure approximately: 5" x 4.75", EX, Herstad Collection.

Good	Excellent	Near Mint
$5-10.00	$30-50.00	$50-75.00

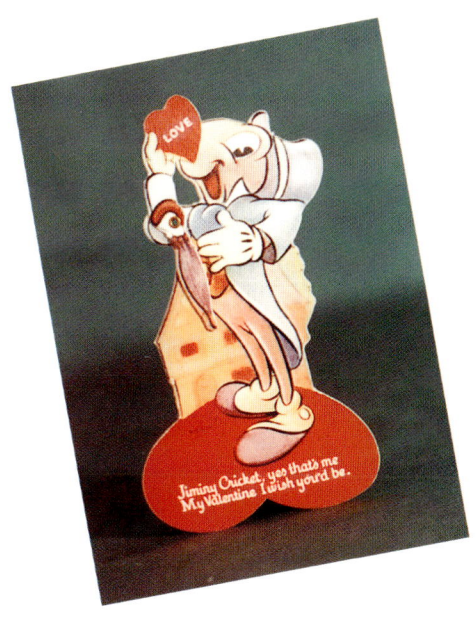

Mickey Mouse and Pluto combination on heart-shaped card, NMF, ©1938, W.D. Ent., made in U.S.A., 5.25" x 5", EX, Herstad Collection.

Good	Excellent	Near Mint
$5.00	$50.00	$75.00

Pinocchio and Geppetto heart-shaped series, NMF, ©1938, W.D. Ent., made in U.S.A., another one in this series pictured on page 113 in *Valentines With Values,* how many in this series are still unknown, 5.25" x 5", EX, Herstad Collection.

Good	Excellent	Near Mint
$5.00	$50.00	$75.00

Pinocchio and Jiminy Cricket on stage coach, Pinocchio in the land of lost children and Geppetto looking after Pinocchio, all NMF,©1939, W.D. Ent., made in U.SA., how many in this series are still unknown, all measure approximately: 7" x 6.5", NM, Herstad Collection.

Good	Excellent	Near Mint
$5.00	$50.00	$75.00

Big-Eyed Walkers, NMF, c. 1920s, PIG, 7.5" x 6" and 5.5" x 4", artist unknown, EX, Kreider Collection.
Bigger version:
Good	Excellent	Near Mint
$5.00	$40.00	$75.00

Smaller version:
Good	Excellent	Near Mint
$2.00	$25.00	$45.00

Walkers, NMF, PIG, c. 1920s, total number in this series are still unknown, all measure approximately 4" x 2.5", EX, Kreider Collection.

Good	Excellent	Near Mint
$2.00	$25.00	$35.00

Disney Fun-Time Valentines in original box (shown), manufactured by Fuld & Company, division of Metropolitan Greetings, made in U.S.A., © Walt Disney Productions, c. 1970s, cards inside box measure 6.25" x 12.25", M, Donated to the Kreider Collection by Fran and Al Childress, Stockton, California.

Good	Excellent	Near Mint
$5.00	$25.00	$50.00

Assorted Valentines in original box, NF, c. 1950s, made in U.S.A., 38 cards sold for 59 cents, M, Kreider Collection.

Good	Excellent	Near Mint
$5.00	$25.00	$35.00

Educator Approved Valentines in original box, NF, c. 1965, manufactured by Doubl-Glo, back of box is also shown, a lot of time and effort went into the making of this box of cards for children so they were politically correct, made in U.S.A., 25 cards sold for 39 cents, M, Kreider Collection.

Good	Excellent	Near Mint
$5.00	$15.00	$15.00

Can of peaches, NF, c. 1940s, made in U.S.A, 4.75" x 3.5", NM, Kreider Collection.

Good	Excellent	Near Mint
$2.00	$10.00	$15.00

12 Valentine cut-outs in original package, NF, made in U.S.A., No. 800, sold for 15 cents, initials on each card: CPC, M, Kreider Collection.

Good	Excellent	Near Mint
$5.00	$10.00	$15.00

Peach bathing beauty, dressed fruit, NF, c. 1940s, made in U.S.A., 4.75" x 3.75", NM, Kreider Collection.

Good	Excellent	Near Mint
$2.00	$10.00	$15.00

Peach and Pear persons, dressed fruit, NF, c. 1940s, made in U.S.A., 4" x 3", NM, Kreider Collection.

Good	Excellent	Near Mint
$2.00	$10.00	$15.00

"The baggage smasher," "Getting tiresome," "Aping the style," and "Widower," NF, all penny dreadfuls, c. early 1900s, all wood blocks, the values of this style of card will vary according to occupation, all measure approximately: 9.5" x 7", EX, Kreider Collection.

Good	Excellent	Near Mint
$3.00	$25.00	$35.00

"Wolf, "Shop Girl," and "Hen-Pecked," NF, all penny dreadfuls, c. mid 1900s, printed in U.S.A., all measure approximately 9.5" x 7.5", EX, Kreider Collection.

Good	Excellent	Near Mint
$2.00	$15.00	$25.00

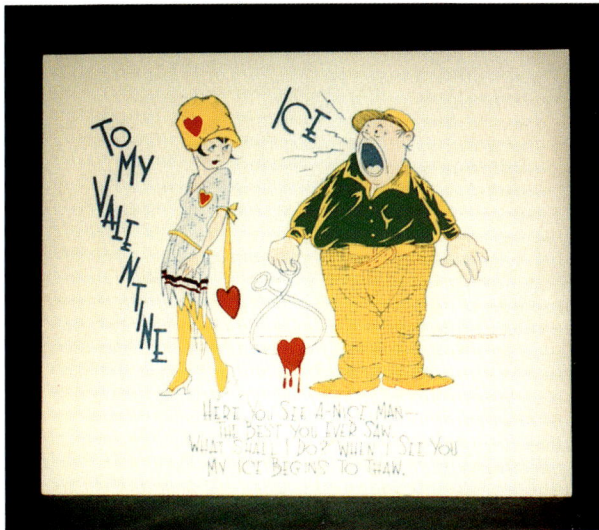

Flapper series, NF, c. 1920s, all printed in U.S.A., all measure approximately 5" x 6", EX, Kreider Collection.

Good	Excellent	Near Mint
$2.00	$15.00	$25.00

"Lucky Lipstick," NF, c. 1930s, printed in U.S.AM. (for other penny dreadfuls see pages 101-111 in *Valentines With Values*), NM, Kreider Collection.

Good	Excellent	Near Mint
$2.00	$15.00	$20.00

"Don't Be a Simp," NF, penny dreadful, c. 1930s, 6.25" x 4.5", NM, Kreider Collection.

Good	Excellent	Near Mint
$2.00	$15.00	$20.00

Chapter Two
♥ Deltiology: the Study of Postcards ♥

Why postcards? A postcard is another style of Valentine to be added to the other styles of cards: dimensional, flat, mechanical-flat, and greeting card. We give our thanks for postcards to a common man who understood the disadvantage of being poor. His name was Rowland Hill, from England, and his proposal to the postal system was entitled: *Post Office Reform; Its Importance and Practicability*. Because of him the Uniform Penny Postage was implemented, therefore paving the way for the cost-effective postcard.

Before the postcard, there was writing paper that could be folded into an envelope or slipped into a separate envelope and carried by the Postman. The charge for this service was determined by the distance the carrier would have to take the letter, therefore putting the burden of paying the postage on the receiver of the letter. The common person would have to turn the letter away, because they would not have enough money to pay for the postage. To make matters worse, Members of Parliament were given free postage as a perk, plus newspapers were delivered free of charge. As with any business, the object was to make money, not to lose it, so the everyday letter would have had to offset the losses in postage.

It was time to look at Hill's proposal seriously. After three years of analyzing the proposal, on January 10, 1840, the Uniform Penny Postage was finally put into effect. On May 1, 1940, the first prepaid official Post Office envelopes and stamps were available in one-cent and two-cent denominations. With this new cost-effective postal change in effect, it was inevitable that this system would spread worldwide. Russia and Finland were the first in 1845 to implement a similar system, with several states in Germany following closely behind. The United States issued their first postal stationery in 1876 for the Philadelphia Centennial Exposition.

All of this paved the way for the cost-effective postcard. October 1, 1869, was the first official day the postcard was born, with credit going to Austria-Hungary. It wasn't until October 1, 1870, that Britain introduced its first postcards, measuring 4 3/8" x 3 1/2", and imprinted them with a halfpenny stamp. Later the size of the postcard would be changed to 4 3/4" x 3", therefore allowing the card to fit evenly within the Postman's bundle of mail.

In the 1860s, the photo card was introduced en masse, with images of works of art, famous people, views of cities and countries and, eventually, even families appearing on these cards. The photographer would travel throughout the streets of cities and towns to capture the real life of the people. The demands for these photographic images were limited to the local people in the towns. This is still true today. Deltiologists (collectors of postcards) are territorial and topically motivated when it comes to adding to their collections. They look for obscure towns, trades, and ethnic groups represented on these photographic essays of our growing nation. Today these cards can demand quite a high premium, depending on the image, photographer, and whether a particular town is still in existence. This is another way for all of us to help preserve history. Once the towns are gone and the photographs are gone, we will have that much less to remind us how America grew and changed as a nation.

Canada, in June 1871, was the first non-European country to issue a postcard, with France, Japan, Italy, Chile, parts of Scandinavia (not the entire country), Romania, Spain, Russia, and the United States following closely behind; all had postal cards by the end of 1874.

It seems there is always an official version and unofficial version when you are dealing with free enterprise. A citizen of the United States known as John Charlton obtained a copyright for an unofficial postal card in 1861; later he transferred the copyright to H. Lipman. So we have Lipman's Postal Card. These cards were actually dated prior to Austria's official version in 1869. It must be noted that Lipman's cards were the first to be sanctioned by a postal authority, even though, technically, they were the unofficial postcard put out by the government postal service. By the way, the word "postcard" must appear on each card to consider it an official postcard.

Initially, postal cards were only allowed to travel within the country in which they were sent. If the post office received cards with extra postage attached, to be sent to another country, the card would immediately be returned to the sender. As with all new ideas, it had to be molded to fit society's needs and desires. This gave way to the development of The General Postal Union. Twenty-two countries comprised the General Postal Union, later known as The Universal Postal Union, with sixteen additional countries added to its roster. This Union allowed the development of a fixed rate of postage to send mail from one country to another. With that in the bag, time for another change, the foreign postcard was born.

As the postcard grew in popularity, the businessmen of the world began to take notice. They decided this would be a wonderful advertising tool for their products, thus the tradecard was born. The tradecard is the precursor of the business card of today. These cards would have printed on them the tradesman's occupation or the product he was offering for sale. They were beautifully executed using the chromolithography printing process, giving each and every company its own distinctive appearance to capture the customer's attention. Sometimes the image was far removed from the type of business the salesmen were trying to promote. A printer would offer several generic images to choose from, then the printer would imprint a company's name and address on the card of choice. As with Valentine cards, tradecards are also sought after by many ephemerists in the market place today.

Another branch of the postal card genre would be the Victorian calling card. These were used for Sunday visits to friends or business associates. Visitors would leave cards that were imprinted or hand written with their names underneath the Victorian die cut scrap of each small card. The ladies of the manor would make an evening out of pasting these cards into an album known as a scrap book. Without TVs and movies to pass the time, this would be their entertainment on cold winter nights. Today we can still find wonderful scrapbooks intact, with all sorts of exquisite die cuts pasted in them.

Postcard collecting grew at a rapid pace, once it caught the public's attention. Publishing companies wanted to make sure that this trend would continue for years to come, so they were always searching for ways to market their own product more effectively. Raphael Tuck and Sons, one of the publishers of postcards (and Valentine cards, etc.), came up with a marvelous idea. The company developed competitions with cash prizes to promote its postcard business. With each competition a different spin would be put on the contest. Basically, whoever had the most Tuck cards would win, either in a series or just in the number of Tuck cards the person owned. Similarly, today the Hallmark company gives points for each dollar spent on a Hallmark card. In return they issue a discount certificate worth a certain dollar value depending upon the points you have accumulated throughout the year.

The postcard had a tremedous effect on society. It was a media outlet for advertising political commentary and a self-promotional tool for a soon-to-be personality in the media. Postcards were basically split into two types: view cards showing a city, street, or town; and subject cards showing images of animals, modes of transportation, beautiful women, and movie stars.

Improving upon an already good thing, the novelty card was added, just as the greeting card companies added Valentine cards. Included within this style of postcard was the mechanical card. These cards had moving parts, such as the ones pictured in this chapter, for instance the kaleidoscope card. Published by Alpha Publishing Company, the kaleidoscope card allowed you to change the images within; the lever type card was pulled to make another image appear. These cards were meant to be played with.

One of the most fascinating mechancial cards ever made was produced by Raphael Tuck & Sons. It was the gramophone card. This card could actually be played on a phonograph at the 78 rpm speed. Tuck produced at least sixteen sets of these cards with four cards per set.

The Continental Series was introduced, depicting famous broadsides, and illustrations from magazines. These were usually printed in a limited edition series of cards. This type of card would promote a particular artist/illustrator and were usually signed by the artist. Due to the limited number of these cards produced, these series are very important to the serious postcard collector. There are some artists you should keep in mind when searching for postcards: Ellen Clapsaddle, Frances Brundage, Rose O'Neill, R.F. Outcault, Leyendecker, Arthur Thiele, and Charles Twelvetrees are among the most important.

Raphael Tuck & Sons were known for their series of postcards. Their first set of cards contained twelve cards with images of London. Each card was imprinted with the title "The Raphael Tuck & Sons View Postcard," numbered one through twelve. As we approach the Golden Age of postcards that endured from the early 1900s to the 1920s, Tuck produced more sets of cards using the chromolithography process with the added technique of embossing some of his cards. Tuck's sets came in either a pack of six or twelve.

Other manufacturers tried to keep up with Tuck's innovative ideas. They had ideas of their own. For an example, postcards that were made to be cut out, such as dressing/paper dolls and their various interchangeable outfits.

Just like Valentine cards, you also had hold-to-light postcards, with a series of cut-out windows that glowed when held up to a light. It looked as though you just switched on the light, or another image would appear that could not be seen with the naked eye.

Of course, manufacturers wanted to have a card for every budget, so they had to produce a less expensive line of novelty postcards. These cards were unusual indeed, they made them out of wood, aluminum, and leather. They added such adornments as real hair, feathers, glitter, miniature and giant cards, etc. This type of card was not very "postman-friendly." The glitter (powdered glass) fell off of the glitter cards onto all of the other mail; the miniature and giant cards could not fit properly into the post carrier's bundles. To help solve these problems, more postal regulations were added.

Originally, you were not allowed to write on the backs of the postcards, as we do today. You would write your message on the front of each card. The vignette would usually be printed on the left-hand side of the card, leaving a small amount of room for the sender's message. In the early 1900s, this started to change when England allowed the address to be written on the back of the card. By then, the image on the front had gradually taken over the whole front area, leaving little room for the address and message. Initially, the cards were not divided. It was not until 1906 to 1907 that the divided back, as we know it today, came into use.

The war brought on other variations of the postcard: wartime humor cards, suffragette cards, embroidered silk patriotic and sentimental cards for our wartime heros. One of the more unique cards I have seen was the embroidered silk patriotic card. These cards were hand embroidered, sometimes they would have a small pocket in them so you could slip a silk hankie in them for a token of love. Due to the high cost of making this type of card, their production was short-lived and only lasted a couple of years in the mid-1900s.

One of the most exquisite uses of color on postcards, was during the art deco period from 1920s to 1940s. A technique called color blocking, was used in which two or more colors that would not normally go together would be combined in an illustration. Black, orange, pink, turquoise, purple, bright green, and silver are just some of the colors that would be found in this art form. Some of the most profound artists of the art deco period are: Carlo Chiostri, Tito Corbells, Achille Mauzan, Umberto Brunelleschi, and M. Montedoro. The art deco postcard as well as the art deco Valentine card are becoming prized by many deltiologists and Valentine collectors today.

As the 1930s arrived, the art deco movement was fading away and the next war was right around the corner. Unfortunately, postcards from the second World War are difficult to find, they were not kept in albums as often as the ones that preceded this war. During World War II postcards reflected the war effort. Most of the population was involved in the war effort, usually working in war related jobs around the clock, and had very little recreational time for putting postcards into albums.

During the next twenty years sending postcards became unfashionable. People had more interest in television and radio. Postcards were still produced, but a lot of them were thrown out, due to lack of interest. These cards that remain will grow in value because of this ephemeral attitude. I cringe to think what will happen to the postcard with all the e-mails, today. Hopefully, with the help of all of the wonderful deltiologists in the world, they will save the postcard from total extinction.

Chromolitho, embossed images, c. early 1900s, Corp. E. Nash, PIG, both cards are part of a series, No. 22, EX, Kreider Collection.

Good	Excellent	Near Mint
$5.00	$10.00	$15.00

"To My Sweethart," glitter card, c. early 1900s, EX, Kreider Collection.
Value of card is unframed:
Good   Excellent   Near Mint
$3.00 $5.00 $10.00

Embossed linen card, PIG, c. 1920s, L & E, No. 7040, EX, Swanson Collection.
Good   Excellent   Near Mint
$1.00 $5.00 $8.00

Colored linen card, border embossed, postally unused, MIG, AS: © H.W.W. or H. L. Woehler of Buffalo, NY, EX, Swanson Collection.
Good   Excellent   Near Mint
$5.00 $10.00 $15.00

Chromolitho embossed cards, AS: Ellen H. Clapsaddle, c. mid 1900s, published by: International Art Pub. Co., PIG, series #601, vertical image and series #4233, both cards were postally used, Note: the use of the same image on both cards, EX, Swanson Collection.

Good	Excellent	Near Mint
$5.00	$10.00	$15.00

Embossed chromolitho card, PIG, c. early 1900s, published by International Art Pub. Co., EX, Kreider Collection.

Good	Excellent	Near Mint
$2.00	$5.00	$10.00

Mechanical chromolitho Clown, PIB, AS, published by E.P. Dutton Co., New York, Ernest Nister, London, does not have a postal back, EX, Renshaw Collection.

Good	Excellent	Near Mint
$10.00	$35.00	$45.00

Postcard with dimension, c. mid 1900s, published by John Winsch, EX, Renshaw Collection.

Good	Excellent	Near Mint
$10.00	$20.00	$30.00

Chromolitho, c. mid 1900s, published by John Winsch, unsigned: S.L. Schmucker Design, NM, Renshaw Collection.

Good	Excellent	Near Mint
$20.00	$40.00	$60.00

Hand colored on silk, published by John Winsch (no copyright), c. mid 1900s, unsigned, S.L.. Schmucker Design. Note: same image used on the other card, NM, Renshaw Collection.

Good	Excellent	Near Mint
$30.00	$60.00	$80.00

Portrait of beautiful lady, PIG, c. early 1900s, design copyright © John Winsch, EX, Kreider Collection.

Good	Excellent	Near Mint
$10.00	$15.00	$25.00

Cupid with human hair, wings are made of spun glass, c. mid 1900s, publisher and artist unknown, NM, Renshaw Collection.

Good	Excellent	Near Mint
$10.00	$20.00	$30.00

Embroidered silk postcard, dated 1915, done in France, NM, Renshaw Collection.

Good	Excellent	Near Mint
$2.00	$8.00	$10.00

Chromolitho card, c. mid 1900s, published by International Art Pub. Co., PIG, series #842, NM, Renshaw Collection.

Good	Excellent	Near Mint
$2.00	$8.00	$10.00

Chromolitho card, c. mid 1900s, no maker, MIG, NM, Renshaw Collection.

Good	Excellent	Near Mint
$2.00	$8.00	$10.00

Fortune Valentine Series, c. mid 1900s, no maker, chromolitho, NM, Renshaw Collection.

Good	Excellent	Near Mint
$2.00	$8.00	$10.00

Chromolitho embossed card, c. mid 1900s, no maker, PIG, NM, Renshaw Collection.

Good	Excellent	Near Mint
$2.00	$8.00	$10.00

Chromolitho embossed card, c. mid 1900s, no maker, PIG, NM, Renshaw Collection.

Good	Excellent	Near Mint
$2.00	$8.00	$10.00

Chromolitho embossed card, c. mid 1900s, published by International Art Pub. Co., PIG, NM, Renshaw Collection.

Good	Excellent	Near Mint
$2.00	$8.00	$10.00

Chromolitho card, postally unused, early 1900s, no maker, #5006 imprinted on front of card, EX, Kreider Collection.

Good	Excellent	Near Mint
$2.00	$10.00	$15.00

Silk heart as center motif, with gold embossed letters and chromolitho peony-type flowers, postally unused, published by John Winsch, PIG, EX, Kreider Collection.

Good	Excellent	Near Mint
$2.00	$10.00	$15.00

Crepe paper heart as center motif with original brass key in center, c. early 1900s, no maker, EX, Smith Collection.

Good	Excellent	Near Mint
$2.00	$5.00	$10.00

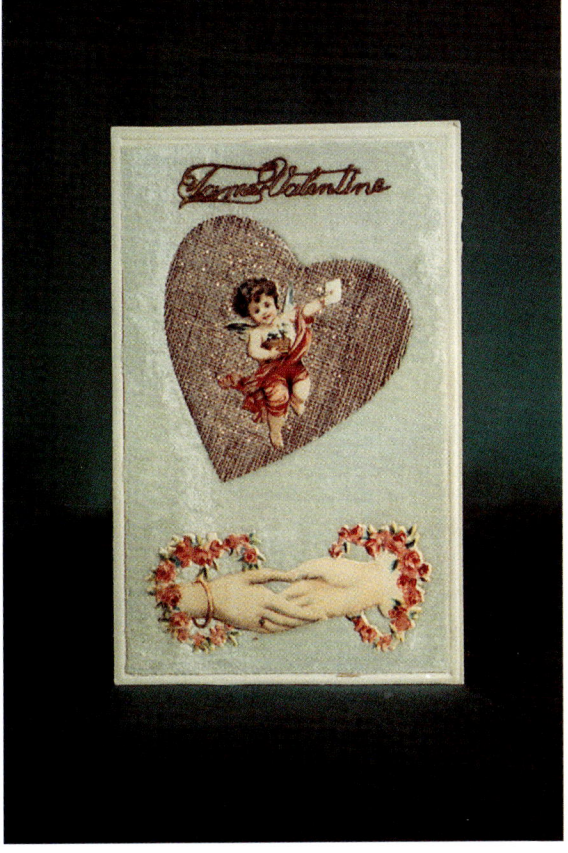

Velour heart as center motif accented with Victorian die cut scraps, embossed gold letters on front of card, c. early 1900s, no maker, NM, Smith Collection.

Good	Excellent	Near Mint
$2.00	$5.00	$10.00

Chromolitho card, c. mid 1900s, no maker, made in U.S.A., G, Kreider Collection.

Good	Excellent	Near Mint
$1.00	$3.00	$5.00

Chromolitho card with open up greeting card effect, c. early 1900s, artist and publisher unknown, PIG, EX, Kreider Collection.

Good	Excellent	Near Mint
$5.00	$10.00	$15.00

Dressed animals, chromolitho embossed card, postally unused, PIG, EX, Kreider Collection.

Good	Excellent	Near Mint
$5.00	$10.00	$15.00

Hold-to-light postcard (w/cut-outs), undivided back, c. 1906, publisher and artist unknown, NM, Renshaw Collection.

Good	Excellent	Near Mint
$20.00	$50.00	$75.00

Mechanical, chromolitho postcard, c. mid 1900s, published by International Art Pub. Co., artist unkown, NM, Renshaw Collection.

Good	Excellent	Near Mint
$5.00	$10.00	$20.00

Flapper-type girl with fan, chromolitho, c. 1920s, maker unknown, EX, Renshaw Collection.

Good	Excellent	Near Mint
$5.00	$10.00	$15.00

Diva sporting fur boa and fur muff, chromolitho, undivided back, copyright 1906, series No. 5, c. mid 1900s, published by Raphael Tuck & Sons, NM, Renshaw Collection.

Good	Excellent	Near Mint
$2.00	$4.00	$8.00

Lady tied up in knots with her pup, c. early 1920s, no maker, made in U.S.A., divided back, postally unused, EX, Kreider Collection.

Good	Excellent	Near Mint
$2.00	$5.00	$8.00

Children with Valentine greetings, c. early 1920s, made by Whitney, Worcester, Mass., undivided back, EX, Renshaw Collection.

Good	Excellent	Near Mint
$1.00	$5.00	$8.00

These colored cards show the same image used differently: the first image was postally used in 1925, the second image does not have a postcard back, but is on the same weight stock. It is cut as a "clever card" (sometimes known as "Klever Kard," a trademark name). When this card is bent back it forms a stand for the image to stand out, EX, Swanson Collection.

Good	Excellent	Near Mint
$2.00	$5.00	$8.00

Roses in four different shades, chromolitho, embossed card, all cards postally unused, c. early 1900s, PIG, EX, Kreider Collection.

Good	Excellent	Near Mint
$5.00	$10.00	$15.00

Kaleidoscope heart, mechanical card, copyright 1910, published by International Art Pub. Co., artist unknown, No. 51810, NM, Renshaw Collection.

Good	Excellent	Near Mint
$15.00	$25.00	$35.00

Native American Series, chromolitho, No. 830, c. early 1900s, AS: Ellen Clapsaddle, EX, Smith Collection.

Good	Excellent	Near Mint
$5.00	$10.00	$15.00

Lady looking for her "Sailor Valentine" at sea, chromolitho, printed in Saxony, Fred S. Howard, printed by Winsch & Co., "Old Sweet Songs" Series, No. 257, designed in England, NM, Kreider Collection.

Good	Excellent	Near Mint
$15.00	$25.00	$35.00

Fairy lady bringing basket of hearts bordered with violets, chromolitho embossed, same image used as booklet in Chapter 3, c. mid-1900s, artist unknown, EX. Renshaw Collection.

Good	Excellent	Near Mint
$5.00	$10.00	$15.00

"Love's Message," chromolitho, postally unused, AS: Ellen Clapsaddle, © Wolf & Co., Phila., EX, Swanson Collection.

Good	Excellent	Near Mint
$5.00	$10.00	$15.00

"Ladies Waiting Room", chromolitho, AS: Ellen Clapsaddle, PIG, painting of image is copyrighted by International Art Pub. Co., Series No. 1827, EX, Swanson Collection.

Good	Excellent	Near Mint
$5.00	$10.0	$15.00

"Leap Year 1912" photo postcard, postally used, copyright, I. Grollvan, exceptional card in the Valentine world, G, Kreider Collection.

Good	Excellent	Near Mint
$15.00	$25.00	$45.00

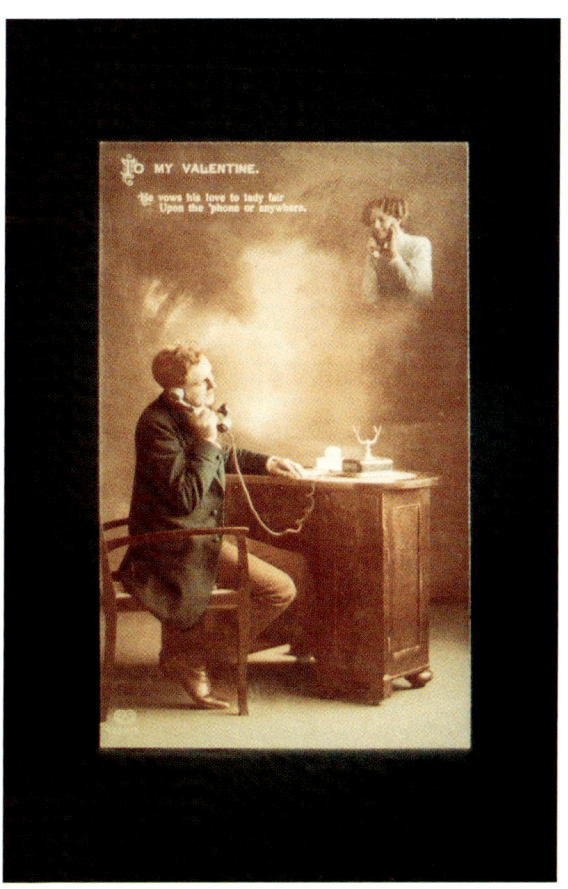

Real photo cards, tinted, all are postally unused, photographers initials on front of card: FAS, these are part of a set or series: #4238/2, #4238/3, #4238/6, and #4238/3, PIG, EX, Swanson Collection.

Good	Excellent	Near MInt
$3.00	$8.00	$10.00

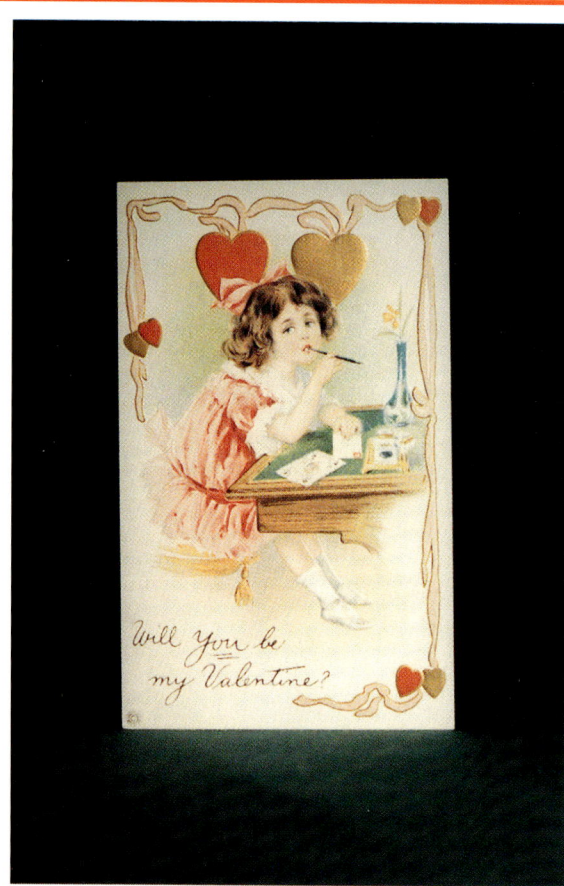

Chromolitho embossed card, all postally unused, c. 1920s, Series from: Stecher Litho Co., Rochester, NY, made in U.S.A., Young lady at writing desk: Series 313 F; Young lady in riding habit: Series 313 E; Clown on bended knee: Series 313 C; Mariachi player: Series 313 D; Young lady curtsying: Series 313 A; M, Kreider Collection.

Good	Excellent	Near Mint
$5.00	$15.00	$20.00

Hand with dove bringing letter, chromolitho, #6707, c. mid-1900s, artist unknown, EX. Kreider Collection.

Good	Excellent	Near Mint
$2.00	$5.00	$8.00

Cherub spinning his web of love, postally unused, copyright trademark shown on back of card, AS: Ellen Clapsaddle, International Art Publishing Co., PIG, Series No. 1235, EX, Kreider Collection.

Good	Excellent	Near Mint
$2.00	$15.00	$25.00

Chapter Three

♥ Other Ephemeral Artifacts ♥

Ephemeral Valentine collectibles are obscure and hard to find collectibles that people like to add to their collections, such as: magazine covers from February 14th, children's books focusing on Valentine's Day, Valentine advertisements, Depression Valentines, decorations, the beautifully colored boxes that the Valentine card-making kits came in, and, of course, the Valentine cachets, from the different post offices around the country.

As you are drawing together your Valentine collections, do not forget to add OEAs, such as: Depression Valentines. They are handmade cards made during the Depression years of the 1930s. They consisted of wallpaper, construction paper, anything that might happen to be around the house. This type of card could also be labeled *"folk art or love tokens."* Some of the earliest Valentines were handmade, dating from the early 1700s. Many art forms were represented in the making of this type of Valentine card: theorem, Fraktur, Scherenschnitte, pin-pricking, and wycinanki. Also included in the folk art category are puzzle Valentines, known as: rebuses, puzzle purses, acrostics, and cryptograms. In this chapter you will find fine examples of Depression Valentines. For more detailed information on these art forms and puzzle Valentines, please consult Chapter One in *Valentines With Values*.

In each book, I like to showcase the cachets from a different city in the United States, with the city name relating to Valentine's Day. In *Valentines With Values* I wrote about Loveland, Colorado, and the wide array of cachets their post office developed over the years. My post office of choice for this book is Valentine, Nebraska.

Valentine, Nebraska, was named after a popular, Congressman who was elected in 1882, E.K. Valentine. It wasn't until 1884 that the town of Valentine became incorporated. The town population was made up primarily of merchants, lawyers, cowboys, and tradesmen. In order to bring more people into the town, they promoted the excellent farm land that was available through advertisements. The ads along with the passing of the Homestead Act worked, bringing many new settlers into the community. Once the new settlers were there, they discovered the land was not rich enough to farm, and a major exodus of thousands of new settlers took place. But all was not lost, the land was perfect for raising cattle.

So thanks to Moses Kinkaid of O'Neill, the Kinkaid Act, was passed in 1904, encouraging ranching instead of farming. Today, Valentine, Nebraska, has a population of around 3,000 people and is a quaint town filled with old western charm. Visitors are always welcomed with a big Valentine, Nebraska, smile!

The first Valentine cachet was designed by Margarete Phelps, Postmistress, in the early 1940s. Valentine, Nebraska, has three cachets that are alternated from year to year. Every year, Valentine's post office receives thousands of cards worldwide for their remailing program. One of the famous return addresses sent to Valentine was from Marilyn Monroe.

In 1980, Japan did a promotion of Valentine, Nebraska, which resulted in thousands of return addresses being remailed to Japan. Along with the remailing program the Chamber of Commerce offers a special Valentine greeting card. Each year, they hold a contest to pick the winning card design from among the local artists of Valentine.

A Valentine collection is not complete without a representation of cachets from each and every town with a name honoring one of the most important days of the year, Valentine's Day! If you would like to participate in the Valentine, Nebraska, remailing program, you may enclose one or many, pre-stamped and pre-addressed Valentine cards in a large first-class envelope and mail it to:

Postmaster: Rick Bordeaux
239 North Hall Street
P.O. Box 9998
Valentine, NE 69201-9998

Your Valentine cards will be removed from the outside envelope and hand stamped with the Valentine cachet, then canceled at the Valentine post office. To ensure delivery by Valentine's Day, U.S. destined mail must be received by February 9th and foreign mail must be received by February 3rd at the Valentine, Nebraska, post office.

If you would like to purchase a Valentine's Day card or cards from Valentine, Nebraska, you may write to:

Valentine Chamber of Commerce
P.O. Box 201
Valentine, NE 69201

The Chamber will be more than happy to get them postmarked for you.

Valentine catalog, c. 1893, by Le Count Bros., San Francisco, California, offerings of comic, lace, and novelty Valentines, shown are two pages from the catalog, NM, Renshaw Collection.

Good	Excellent	Near Mint
$50.00	$125.00	$225.00

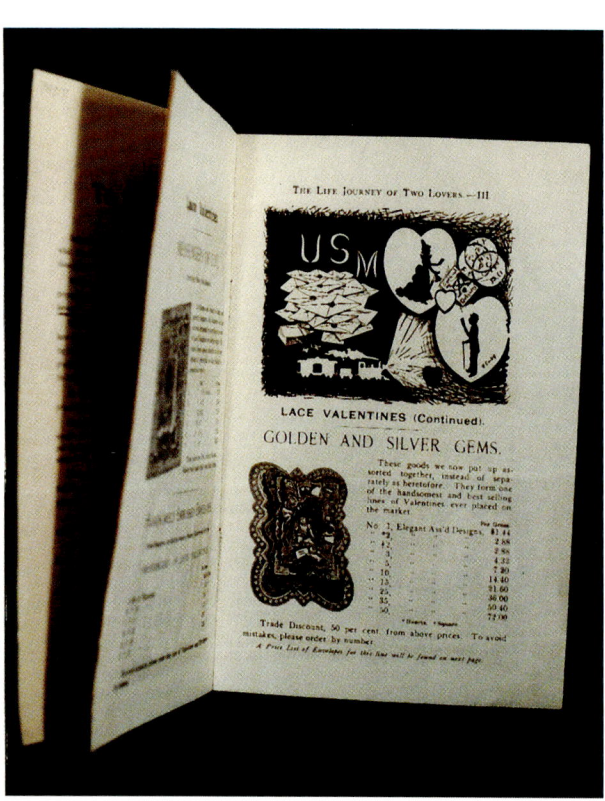

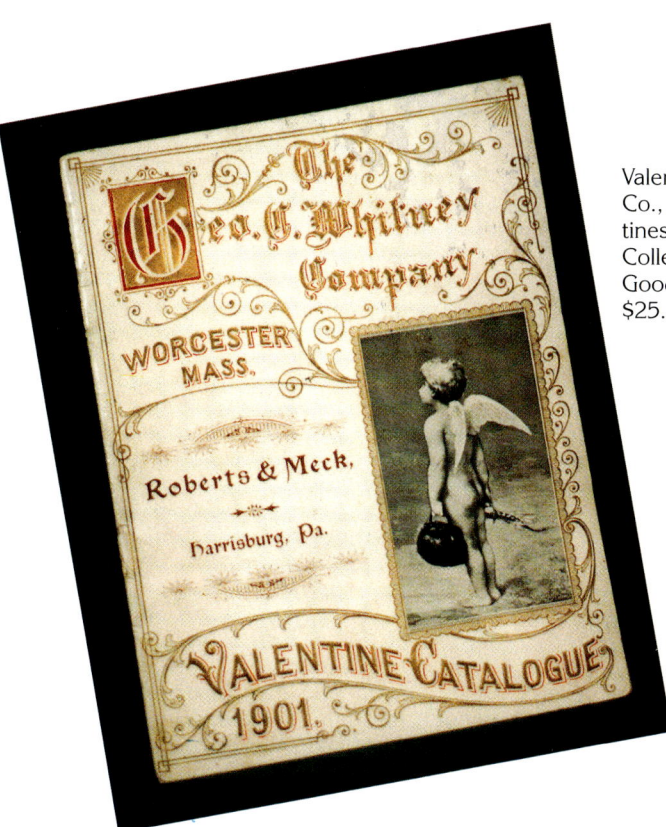

Valentine catalog, c. 1901, manufactured by The Geo. C. Whitney Co., Worcester, Mass., offerings from booklets to novelty Valentines, Roberts & Meck, Harrisburg, Pa., 7.75" x 6", EX, Kreider Collection.

Good	Excellent	Near Mint
$25.00	$75.00	$125.00

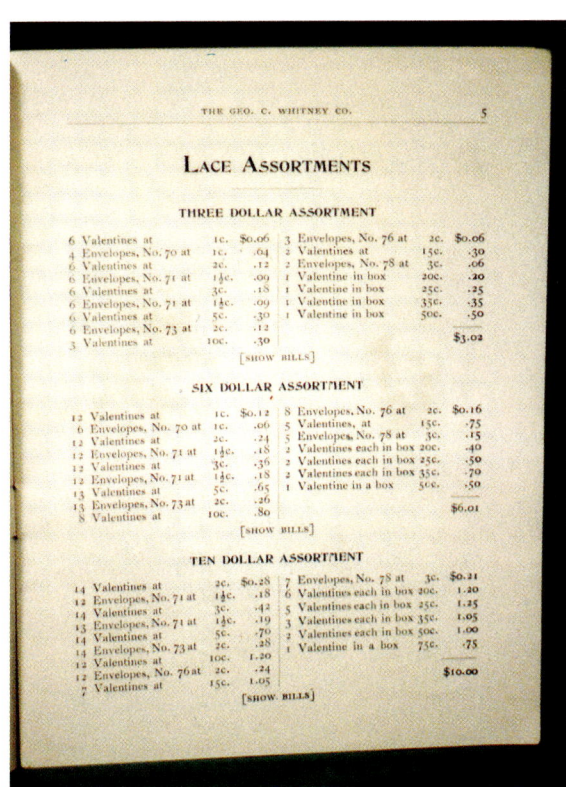

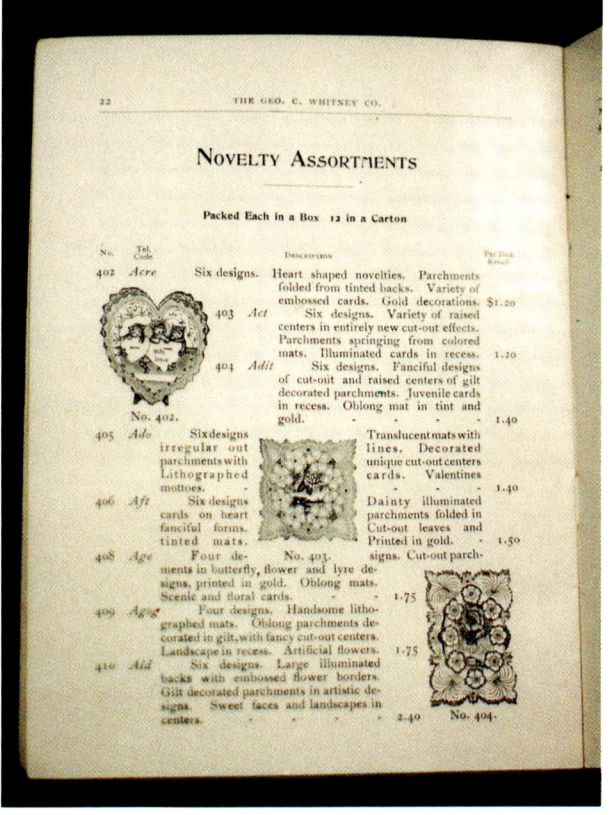

Advertising sampler, c. early 1900s, from Butler & Kelley Company, 26 Beekman Street, New York City, N.Y., manufacturers of and headquarters for folders, ball programs, invitations, menus, tickets, tally cards, tassels, calendars, advertising cards, 4" x 4", EX., Kreider Collection.

Good	Excellent	Near Mint
$5.00	$25.00	$50.00

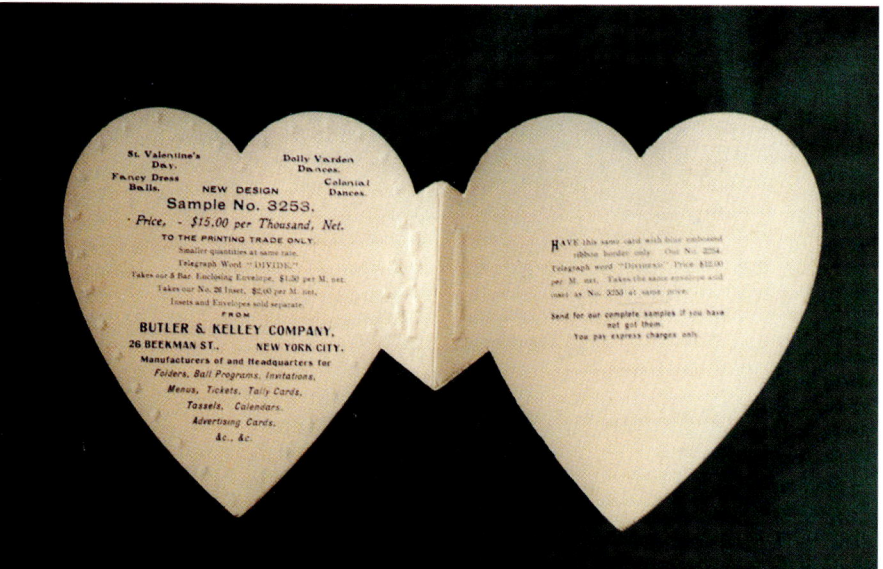

Cupid's Book of Good Counsel, c. 1920s, San Francisco and Sacramento, these two books were given to future brides once they announced their engagements. The Chamber of Commerce in the major cities of California put these books together. As of now California is the only known state to offer *Cupid's Book*. Each book is filled with local merchants advertising their products for the home, recipes, banks, how to remove spots, etc. Currently, major department stores such as Bloomingdales give out such a book advertising everything they have for the bride's future home. 9.25" x 6", EX, Kreider Collection.

Good	Excellent	Near Mint
$10.00	$50.00	$75.00

The Heart of New York City, souvenir booklet with original tassel, patented 1907, this was postally used; on the back to and from are imprinted, original 1-cent postage stamp on the back, measures 3" x 3", when it is opened a series of black-and-white photographs of landmarks in New York City pull out, measuring to 22", NM, Smith Collection.

Good	Excellent	Near Mint
$10.00	$25.00	$50.00

World War II Valentine card from Holland, c.1945, no maker, 5.75" x 4", EX, Smith Collection.

Good	Excellent	Near Mint
$10.00	$50.00	$75.00

112

American Valentine Cards, advertising piece, c. 1940s, F, 6.25" x 5", NM, Kreider Collection.

Good	Excellent	Near Mint
$5.00	$10.00	$15.00

Berkshire Stockings, advertising piece, F, with easel back, artist signed: Jervis, No. on the bottom left hand corner: 21519, 9" x 7", M, Kreider Collection.

Good	Excellent	Near Mint
$5.00	$25.00	$50.00

McDonald's Valentine Gift Giving Certificates, © 1998, Oakbrook, Il, The McDonaldland characters, names and designs are registered Trademarks of the McDonald's Corporation, printed in U.S.A. 3" x 4.5", M, Kreider Collection.
No value other then purchase price at this time.

Valentine's Day book, *Happy Times with Jack and Jane,* published by Lyons & Carnahan, illustrated by Vera Stone Norman, ©1934-1939, 7.25" x 5.25", NM, Smith Collection.

Good	Excellent	Near Mint
$15.00	$50.00	$75.00

Valentine seals, 25 in package, made by: Dennison's Manufacturing Co., The Tag Makers, Trademark reg., made in U.S.A., box measures: 1.5" x 2.5", EX, Kreider Collection.

Good	Excellent	Near Mint
$1.00	$5.00	$10.00

Cinderella carriage, roof, sides, and seats made entirely of HCPP, c. late 1940s-early 1950s, no maker, possibly center piece, 11.5" x 11.5" x 10", NM, Kreider Collection.

Good	Excellent	Near Mint
$5.00	$95.00	$150.00

Seventy red hearts, cupids and darts in original wrapper, c. 1920s, no maker, package measures 4" x 5.5", M, Kreider Collection.
Good	Excellent	Near Mint
$1.00	$5.00	$10.00

Valentine favor cups, MF, made in U.S.A, shown with heart up and shown down, each one is collapsible, c. 1920s, published by International Art Publishing Co., 4.75" high x 1.5" wide, EX, Kreider Collection.
Good	Excellent	Near Mint
$5.00	$10.00	$15.00

California Rasin, "Be Mine," c. 1988, EX, Kreider Collection.
Good	Excellent	Near Mint
$2.00	$5.00	$10.00

Valentine Kit, c.1920s, made by F. & Co., Inc., NY, printed in U.S.A., contents: lace hearts, red shapes, lace papers, everything you need to make the perfect Valentine card, scraps inside were PIG, the two cards shown are fine examples of cards that could be made form this type of kit, box measures: 7.75" x 5", EX, Kreider Collection.

Good	Excellent	Near Mint
$5.00	$25.00	$45.00

Original Valentine material boxes, c. 1920s, no maker, both had contents for making lace Valentines. It is very unusual to find the empty boxes since they were usually thrown out, boxes measure: 7" x 8.25", EX, Kreider Collection.

Good	Excellent	Near Mint
$5.00	$25.00	$50.00

Beautifully colored envelope, postally used, c. 1920s, no maker, similar to Whitney made cards, measures 9.5" x 10.75", EX, Kreider Collection.

Good	Excellent	Near Mint
$5.00	$15.00	$25.00

"Leap Year Card," F, rare, c. 1920s, no maker, art deco type card, 5.25" x 3.5", NM, Kreider Collection.
Good	Excellent	Near Mint
$10.00	$50.00	$75.00

The Heart's Gift, Valentine booklet, with mono-litho images inside, with original silk cord attached, embossed chromolitho cover, Victorian scrap attached as motif on front of card, 5" x 4", NM, Kreider Collection.
Good	Excellent	Near Mint
$5.00	$25.00	$35.00

"Depression" Valentines were made from anything one could make a card out of. (Note: see hankie "Rebus" pictured "Well You Be Mine?" 1933), wallpaper, scraps of construction paper, this also could be called the "poor man's" Valentine, not everyone could afford to spend money on cards so they would lovingly take materials they had around the house to make some of the most beautiful Valentines, most of the time these were thrown out. A lot of the wallpaper Valentines were done during the Depression, EX, Kreider Collection.
No values available at this time.

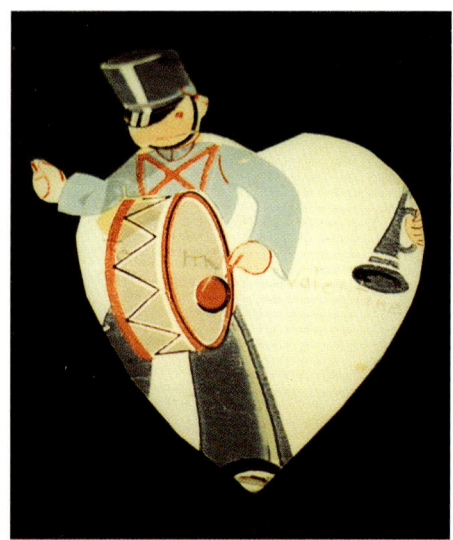

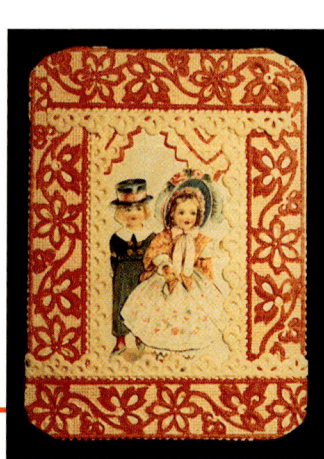

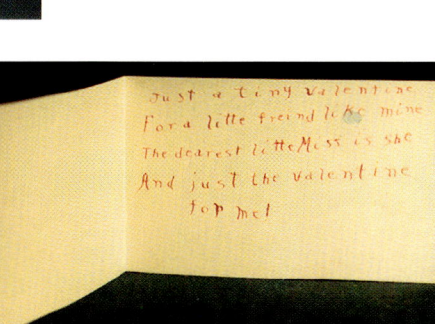

Valentine card booklet, angel children images used on front of card, with orginal silk cord, chromolitho, embossed, c. early 1900s, published by Raphael Tuck & Sons, Germany, back of card shown with Tucks logo printed on the back of card, along with initials C & E, 4" x 4", NM, Kreider Collection.

Good	Excellent	Near Mint
$5.00	$35.00	$45.00

Fairy with basket full of hearts, GC booklet, image also used on postcard, see chapter on Postcards, 6" x 4", NM., Renshaw Collection.

Good	Excellent	Near Mint
$3.00	$15.00	$25.00

Valentine, Nebraska's, cachets and a sampling of greeting cards. Card pictured on the far left–1998 official Valentine, artist Vicky Cumbow; card top center–1993 official Valentine, artist Gina Witte Feller; card bottom center–1992 official Valentine, artist Dave Price; card far right–T. In/Girl Scouts. Top three are the cachets that the post office alternates from year to year. In the middle a message from the Chamber of Commerce: Just send $5.00 to Chamber of Commerce, PO Box 201, Valentine, NE 69201. "You can use up to two lines for a message, and we'll send your official Valentine with our special cachet and postmark from Valentine, Nebraska.

Cachets dated 1940s-1950s:

Good	Excellent	Near Mint
$5.00	$10.00	$15.00

Cachets dated 1960s-1970s:

$2.00	$5.00	$8.00

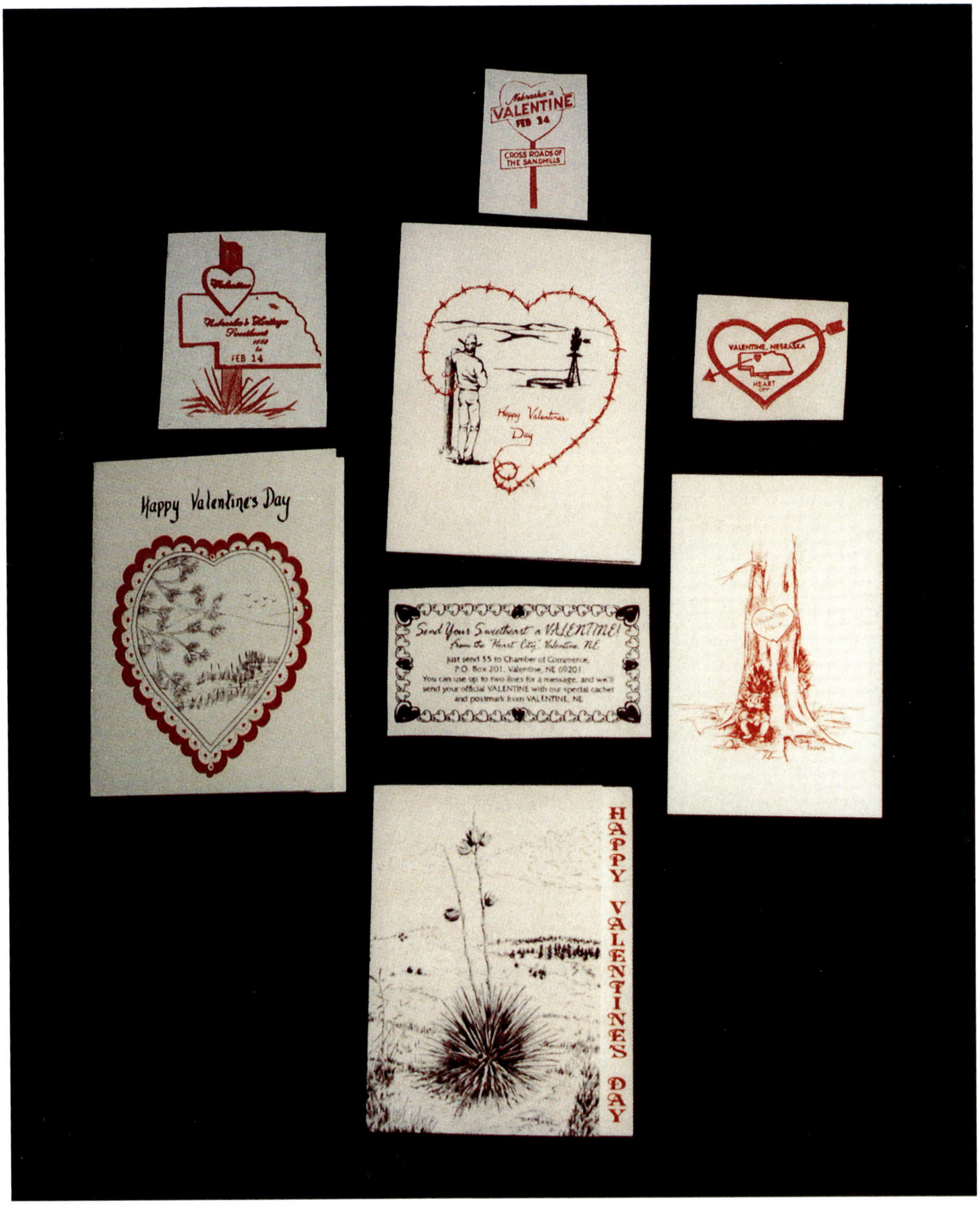

Acquaintance Cards, twelve cards to a pack, sold for 10 cents, an example of which is printed on one of the cards (second card shown): "My Dear Creature" and "If you, would allow me the privilege of escorting you home, I should consider it too awfully all but" or (fourth card shown with boot, gun, and bull dog; it states the following: "Dear Miss: I will risk everything depicted here if you will permit me to see you as far as the gate, Yours Very Truly," EX, Kreider Collection.

Values are for complete set of 12 cards:

Good	Excellent	Near Mint
$5.00	$15.00	$25.00

124

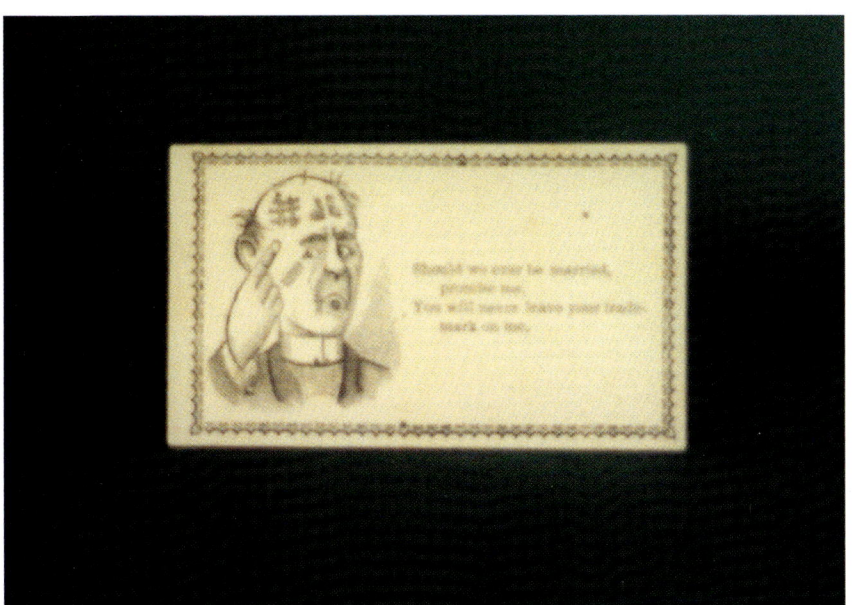

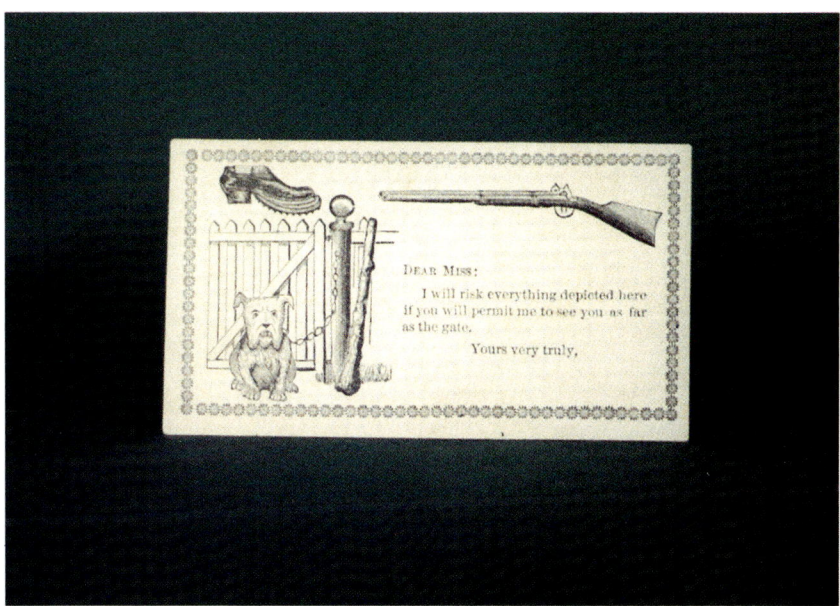

♥ Third Top 10 Most Asked Questions ♥

1. Why is there such a wide range of values for one card?
This question and answer bears repeating time and time again!
Unfortunately, the value of Valentine cards will never be "cut and dry!" As with all collectibles, there are so many variables, and when you are dealing with paper, it becomes more difficult. In the beginning there were six qualifying specifications to consider when calculating the value for a Valentine card: condition, size, age, artist-signed, manufacturer, and category—a seventh one must be added, location. *Remember: A price range always reflects the accessibility and demand of the artifact you are evaluating.* Please refer to the Usage Guide in this book for a further understanding of the range in prices.

2. What Valentine cards do you consider to be the most difficult to find?
G-Man (with the badge attached) and the Monoply game card.

3. Can the chromolithography printing process be duplicated today?
Yes, but it is just too expensive to print cards in this manner today. Each color on a card requires one stone per color. In other words, if you need twelve colors on one card that means twelve stones. When engraving the image onto the stone this requires quite a challenge for the artist/illustrator, since they must engrave the image in reverse onto each stone. For more information on lithography and chromolithography refer to Chapter I in *Valentines With Values*.

4. How do you identify a "series" or "set" of cards?
Sometimes the "set" or "series" of cards will be numbered on the back of each card. Unfortunately, this is not always the case. In some instances you must depend on your keen awareness of an artist's style and theme illustrated on a grouping of cards.

5. Will there ever be a time when the Valentines that are placed into the very good and poor condition levels increase in value?
Yes, as the accessibility and demand of a card is established, this will help to elevate the price of cards placed in these types of conditions.

6. How much did Valentine cards sell for in the 1800s?
Retailers could buy cards by the gross for a penny, but you could also pay $75 for one card in the mid-1800s, priced for the affluent. Esther Howland was known for making special cards in the $50–$75 price range. Please refer to *Valentines With Values* for more information on this subject.

7. What is ephemera?
Anything of printed matter that was meant to be thrown away within 24 hours. It comes from the Mayfly that is born, breeds, and dies within 24 hours. Examples of ephemera would be: ticket stubs, boardsides, tradecards, receipts, baggage labels, etc. Please note: There are several definitions of ephemera, but I find this one to be the purest.

8. How should I catalog my collection?
That depends on the individual collection. If artist-signed cards are the primary focus, then I would suggest you would started cataloging by each artist. If manufacturers are of particular interest, I would start with the different manufacturers. *Valentines With Values, One Hundred Years of Valentines,* and *Valentines for the Eclectic Collector* will give you a definite direction on categorizing your collection.

9. Could you please give us a list of pre-20th century manufacturers and publishers of Valentine cards?
Arthur Ackermann, Rudolph Ackermann, Rudolph Ackerman, Jr., Joseph Addenbrooke, American Valentine Co., J. Andrews, Baldwin & Gleason, Caldwell Benbow & Son, Berlin & Jones, Edward Bollans & Co., Bowles, Bullard Art Pub. Co., T.H. Burke, Robert Canton, R. Carr, Catnach Press, A. Cortman Cox, Thomas De La Rue, De Marson H., Dobbs, Bailey & Co., Dobbs, Kidd & Co., Pasqual Donaldson, W. H. Elliott, Elton, John Evans, Abraham Fisher, T. Frere, Thomas Goode, Goode Bros., Alfred Gray, H. Harwood, G. S. Haskins & Co., Charles P. Huestis, Esther Howland, S.A. Howland, G. Ingram, Jonathan King, Jonathan King, Jr., George Kershaw & Son, Le Blond & Co., Edward Lloyd, Charles Magnue, Joseph Mansell, Albert Marks, J.L. Marks, Richard Marsh, McLoughlin Bros., George Meek, David Mossman, Mrs. Mossman, Mullord Bros., Dean & Munday, N.E.V.Co., Ernest Nister, Obpacher, A. Park, Louis Prang, J. V. Quick, Eugene Rimmel, Rock Bros., H.A. Sanders, G. Smeeton, George Snyder, Thomas Stevens, T. W. Strong, Benjamin Sulman, Edward Taft, Jotham Taft, Torond, Raphael Tuck & Sons, Fred Turner, Marcus Ward & Co., Westwood, Edward Whaites, John Windsor & Sons, J. T. Wood & Co., and James Wrigley.

10. Do you have a list of 20th century manufacturers for us to look for?
This is a partial list: Ambassador Cards, American Greeting Cards, A Novo Laugh, The Barker Co., The Beistle Co., The Buzza Cardozo, The Buzza Co., Campbell Art Co., Carrington Co., Doubl-Glo, The Fairfield Line, H. Fishlove & Co., Gibson, Golden Bell Greeting Cards, Hall Bros., Hallmark, Louis Katz, Norcross, Paramount, The Pastel Co., Rosen Company, Rust Craft, Steiner Litho Co., Thompson-Smith Co., The P.F. Volland Co., Whitman Publishing Co., Whitney, H. L. Woehler.

♥ Glossary ♥

ACROSTIC: a verse where a series of words of equal length are arranged to read the same horizontally or vertically.
AIR BRUSHED: a fine spray of paint applied to HCPP or to a card to give it a varied shade effect.
ANGEL: one of an order of spiritual beings that are attendants and messengers of God.
AQUATINT: a method of etching a printing plate so that the tones similar to watercolor can be reproduced.
ART DECO: an art style of the 1920s through 1940s, expressed by using bold outlines, and streamlined and rectilinear forms.
ART NOUVEAU: art style of the late 19th century, expressed by using waving and leafy type lines.
ARTIST-SIGNED: the artist signs his or her original piece of art work and the manufacturer then reproduces that art work onto a card, resulting in an artist-signed card.
BY-LINE: when the publisher gives the artist credit for his or her illustration by imprinting the artist's name (in block style) along with the name of the ...isher on each card printed. (This is not the artist's actual signature reproduced as with the artist-signed cards that have the actual signature of the artist imprinted on the card.)
CACHET: a design or inscription on an envelope to commemorate a postal or philatelic event.
CARICATURE: an exaggerated image that resembles another image; a look-alike, but exaggerated features.
CELLULOID: an artificial substance composed mostly of cellulose and vegetable fiber. The compound is molded by heat and pressure to the desired shape. It is often used as a substitute for ivory, bone, etc.
CHERUB: one of the second highest order of Angels; a picture or statue of a child's head with wings.
CHOKED TO DEATH: too much gooppety-goop unattractive, too many ribbons, knots, and bows.
CHROMOLITHOGRAPH: a colored picture printed from a series of stones or plates.
CLIFFHANGER: a continuous adventure serial, each episode ends with a suspenseful situation.
COMIC CHARACTER: a cartoon-like individual or animal in a comic strip or cartoon.

♥ Bibliography ♥

BOOKS

Darton, Mike, *Art Deco,* North Dighton, Ma., JG Press, 1996.
Hadfield, John, *The Saturday Book #26,* London, England, Hutchinson of London, 1966.
Hake, Ted, *Hake's Guide to Comic Character Collectibles,* Radnor, Pa., Wallace-Homestead Book Company, 1993.
Heller, Jules, *Print Making Today,* Los Angeles, Ca., Holt, Rinehart and Winston, Inc., 1958.
Horn, Maurice, *100 Years of American Newspaper Comics,* Avenel, N.J., Random House, 1996.
Kreider, Katherine, *Valentines With Values,* Atglen, Pa., Schiffer Publishing, 1996.
—, *One Hundred Years of Valentines,* Atglen, Pa. Schiffer Publishing, 1999.
Lee, Ruth Webb, *The History of Valentines,* Batsford, 1952.
Mashburn, J.L., *Fantasy Postcards,* Enka, N.C., Colonial House Publishers, 1996.
Microsoft, Encarta® 96 Encyclopedia®, ©1993-1995, Microsoft Corporation™. All rights reserved. ©Funk & Wagnalls Corporation. All rights reserved.
Nicholson, Susan Brown, *The Encyclopedia of Antique Postcards,* Radnor, Pa., Wallace-Homestead Book Company, 1994.
Staff, Frank, *The Valentine & Its Origin,* London, England, Frederick A. Praeger, 1969.
Willoughby, Martin, *A History of Postcards,* London, England, Bracken Books, 1994.

ARTICLES

Bird, Carol, "Louder and Funnier for Cupid in 31 Valentines," San Francisco, Ca., *San Francisco Chronicle,* 1931.
Emerson, Marion W., "Hearts and Darts," New York, N.Y., *Avocations,* 1938.
Hill, Jeffrey, "Valentine Collectibles," Oakland, Ca., *Antique Journal,* 1994.
Kreider, Katherine, "Valentines An Era Gone By," *Collectors Showcase,* 1991.
—, "Valentines What to Look For," Iowa, *Barr's Postcard News,* 1992.
—, "Historical Hearts," Middleton, Wis., Pleasant Company, 1997.
—, "Comic Valentines," *Collectors Showcase,* Pleasant Company, 1998.

♥♥♥♥♥♥♥♥♥♥♥♥♥♥♥♥♥♥♥

♥ Index ♥

Advertising
    American Greetings, 27, 113
    Avon, 28
    Ballyhoo, 35
    Berkshire Stockings, 113
    Collier's, 34
    Chicklets, 29
    Cigarette, 36, 37
    Chocolate, 27
    Frigidaire, 31
    Gum, 28
    McDonalds, 113
    Morton Salt, 36
    Nestlé's, 27
    Pillsbury, 36
    Soap Powder, 31
    Whitney, 96
Artists
    Buell, Marjorie Henderson, 10, 39
    Outcault, R.F., 8
    Scott, J.G., 9
    Twelvetrees, Charles, 23, 24
Big-eyed Children, 72, 73
    Walkers, 72, 72
Black Valentines, 28
    Novelty, 28
Celluloid, 12
Comic Characters
    Betty Boop, 9
    Buster Brown, 8, 10
    Ella Cinders, 61
    Dennis the Menace, 10, 63
    Dick Tracy, 9, 10, 43
    Felix the Cat, 10, 38
    Grandpa Foxy, 10, 37
    Henry, 10
    Jiggs, 40
    Lil' Abner, 38
    LuLu, 10, 39
    Mickey and Minnie Mouse, 9, 43, 44, 74
    Moon Mullins, 10, 37
    Popeye, 10, 40
    Snookums, 10, 40
    Superman, 11, 43
    Wonder Woman, 11, 42
Depression
    Folk art, 120, 121
    Wall paper, 120, 121
Disney
    Clarabell, 68
    Cleo, 68
    Dioramas, 65
    Jiminy Cricket, 69
    Pinocchio, 69-71
    Seven Dwarfs, 9, 64-67, 74
    Snow White, 9, 64-66, 74,
Fireman, 44
Flower Children, 47, 48
Gum Cards, 28, 29
HCPP
    Novelty, 14-16, 17
Movie, Radio, and TV Personalities
    James Cagney, 41
    Jimmy Durante, 42
    Charlie McCarthy, 19
    Joe Penner, 42
    Rudi Vallee, 41
Novelty, 8-82
    Celluloid, 12
    Fan, 17, 18
    Finger Puppet, 21
    Gift-Giving, 19, 20, 27
    Guitar, 12
    HCPP, 14-17
    Lollipop Cards, 19, 20
    Love-o-Grams, 23
    Paper Doll, 11, 25, 26
    Penny Dreadfuls, 79-82
    Plastic Eyes, 21, 22
    Punch-Out Cards, 25, 26
    Puzzle, 30
    Pyroxylin, 13
Nursery Rhymes
    Alice in Wonderland, 61
    Cinderella, 54, 55
    Hansel and Gretel, 55
    Jack Horner, 55
    Jack In the Beanstalk, 56
    Little Bo Beep, 62
    Little Red Riding Hood, 54
    Peter Pumpkin Eater, 62
    Pied Piper, 56
    Puss 'n' Boots, 56
    Raggedy Ann and Andy, 62
    Three Bears, 55
    Three Blind Mice, 58
    Wizard of Oz, 9, 58, 59, 60
    Winnie the Pooh, 64
OEAs
    Acquaintance Cards, 124
    Advertising Sampler, 110
    Cachets, 107, 123
    California Raisin,
    Catalogs, 108, 109
    Cupid's Book of Good Counsel, 111
    Depression, 120, 121
    Favor Cups, 116
    Valentine Kits, 117, 118
    Valentine, Nebraska, 107, 123
Paper Doll
    Dressed, 25, 26
Penny Dreadfuls, 79-82
Postcards, 83-106
    Artist-Signed, 87
    Clappsaddle, Ellen, 87, 100, 102, 106
    Dressed Animals, 94
    Embroidered, 90
    Hold-to-Light, 95
    International Art Pub. Co., 87, 90, 92, 100, 106
    Leap Year, 102, 119
    Mechanical, 95
    Nister, Ernest, 88
    Schmucker, S.L., 88, 89
    Tuck, Raphael, 22, 37, 84, 96, 122
    Winsch, John, 88, 89, 93, 101
Scott, J.G., 9
Scouts, 49
    Brownie, 49
    Cub, 49
Transportation, 24
Tuck, Raphael, & Sons, 22, 37, 84, 96, 122
Whitney, George C., 96

COMIC STRIP: a group of cartoons in a narrative series.
COMIC VALENTINE: a card that makes you laugh, a card not to be taken seriously, also may have a character from a newspaper comic strip on it.
COPPERPLATE: a print made from an etched or engraved copper plate.
COTE: shelter or shed for small animals, birds etc.
COURT CARD SIZE: one of the earliest sizes of postcards.
CRYPTOGRAM: a hidden message by using symbols or a code.
CUPID: god of Love, son of Jupiter and Venus, is represented as a winged boy.
CURATOR: a person in charge of an exhibit or museum.
DAGUERREOTYPE VALENTINE: a card with a photo produced on a silver or silver-copper plate used as the center motif.
DELTIOLOGY: the study of postcards.
DIE CUT: the process of cutting paper into different shapes and designs, achieved by using a die.
DIMENSIONAL: measurement of length, width, and depth, can have more than one dimension.
DIORAMA: a scene that is revealed from a distance through an opening.
DIVIDED BACK: when the back of a postcard is separated into two parts, one side for the message and the other side for the address.
DRESDEN: city in Germany on the Elbe River, known for its manufacturing of gold and silver Victorian scraps and holiday ornaments during the 18th century (Saxony).
DEPRESSION CARDS: any handmade card during the Depression era, 1930s, they were made of anything possible, from wall paper to construction paper.
EASEL BACK: a support or upright made of cardboard attached to the back of the card.
EMBOSSED: decorated with a design pattern, etc., that is higher than the surface of the card.
EPHEMERA: anything of printed matter that was meant to be thrown away within 24 hours. (There are several definitions of ephemera, but I find this one to be the purest definition.) It comes from the Mayfly that is born, breeds and dies in a 24 hour time frame. Examples of ephemera would be: ticket stubs, receipts, boardsides, cigar labels, etc.
EPHEMERIST: one who collects ephemera.
ETHNIC: large groups of people with common traits, customs, language, or social views.
FLAT: smooth or level surface.
GILDED: to overlay with a skin-like coating, i.e., gold leaf.
GOLDEN AGE: a period of time when a product has achieved its peak of popularity or sales.
GREETING CARD: a piece of paper folded either horizontally or vertically with either a hand written message or printed message inside.
GRUSS AUS: translated from German, Greetings From.
HONEY COMB PAPER PUFF: tissue paper made into an accordion type paper imitating a bee's honeycomb.
KALEIDOSCOPE: a variegated changing pattern or scene.
LITHOGRAPH: picture, print, etc., made from a flat, specially prepared stone or metal plate.
LOVE TOKEN: anything given from the heart and soul of the giver. The gift could be finely crafted by the giver or purchased from a retail shop. Love tokens could represent anything from porcelain pitchers to a walnut shell with initials carved into the shell.
MECHANICAL: anything with one or more moving part.
MONOCHROMATIC: these are lithographs with one color, either black or brown.
NOVELTY: cards that have a playful or useful item attached or incorporated into the card, such as: perfume, puzzles, linen hankies; unique in style. Novelty cards can also have a comic character or movie personality depicted on them.
OILETTE TRADEMARK: reproductions of oil paintings in realistic color and simulated brush strokes produced on postcards, came in sets of six.
PAPROTAMIA: a art form of making a cobweb Valentine, these were hand cut into a continuous web.
PAPROTYPE: a tough translucent imitation parchment, made by treating paper with a sulfuric acid bath.
PAPYROTYPE: a photolithographic process in which the picture to be reproduced is first printed upon paper and then transferred to the stone or zinc.
PIN PRICK: a shallow hole or mark made with a pin or sharp instrument.
POSTCARD: a one piece card to be delivered through the postal system with a written message on the back.
PYROXYLIN: earliest form of celluloid, yellows with age, fairly light weight (pre-celluloid). A soluble form of cellulose nitrate used in plastic compounds in the arts.
QUARTO: four Valentines would be cut from one piece of paper resulting in the size of four 8" x 10" sheets.
REAL PHOTO CARD: produced from a real photograph onto a photograph paper with a pre-printed postcard back.
REBUS: a riddle represented with pictures or syllables in sound.
SCHERENSCHNITTE: intricate paper cut work done by hand.
SERIES: a grouping of cards that are done by the same artist and printed by the same company.
SETS: cards that came in packets and had four, six, eight, or twelve to a packet. They also were merchandise individually, and usually done by the same artist.
SILHOUETTE: an outline of a person or image cut out from a dark piece of paper, usually done in black, also can be hand drawn onto a piece of paper with ink.
STANDARD SIZE: for postcards: 3.5" x 5".
SUBJECT POSTCARDS: cards with an image depicting topical themes, such as: transportation, animals, beautiful women.
SYNDICATION: to sell a comic strip or cartoon, to one major company for the sole purpose of having the strip or cartoon to appear in many publications and/or periodicals at one time.
TIN TYPE PHOTO OR FERROTYPE: a positive photograph made by a collodion process on a thin iron plate having a darkened surface, when this process is finished the photo has a glossy appearance to it.
TRADECARD: yesterday's business card, used to advertise a company's product or business.
UNCIRCULATED: never used, never opened, the equivalent to mint and in the box.
VALENTINE: a greeting card or small gift sent on Valentine's Day, February 14th; a sweetheart chosen on this day; Saint Christian Martyr of the third century, named, Valentinus.
VENUS: the goddess of beauty and mother of love. Sparrows and doves were most often used to pull her chariot.
VICTORIA: a low four-wheeled pleasure carriage for two, with a calash top and a raised seat in front for the driver or an open passenger automobile with a calash top that usually extends over the rear seat only.
VICTORIAN: pertaining to the reign of Queen Victoria, 1837 to 1901.
VICTORIAN SCRAP: pieces of paper usually embossed and using the chromolithography process; resembling flowers, children, baskets, wreaths, trellises, etc. These scraps were used to embellish cards and ornaments, and usually produced on sheets, then cut apart into individual pieces.
VIEW CARDS: postcards with images of the world around us, such as: cities, towns, streets, train depots, bridges and so on.
WATERMARK: a marking in paper resulting from differences in thickness, produced by the pressure of a projecting design in the mold, visible when the piece of paper is held to the light.
W.D.ENT.: Walt Disney Enterprises, was used prior and during the 1930s.
W.D.P.: Walt Disney Productions, was used after the 1930s.
WOODCUT: is the art form of carving an image into a plank or wood block and often printed by hand.
WOOD ENGRAVING: the wood engraving is cut into the end grain.